WALKING THE WALK

A Karma Yoga Manual

SWAMI TYAGANANDA

Contents

Preface

My mother presented me with a few small books of Swami Vivekananda when I was ten. Looking back, I am amused by how quickly I became attached to those books, since at that age I understood very little of the ideas and ideals presented in them. As years rolled along, I continued to read Vivekananda's books, gradually moving on to his set of *Complete Works*—and I have continued to read them to this day. What little I have understood of life is mostly from Vivekananda's words and to him I owe everything.

Spread over nine volumes, Vivekananda's *Complete Works* are a collection of his lectures, class talks, interviews, conversations, letters, and writings. It is helpful to analyze the nature of its contents. By far the largest segment of the *Complete Works* is the transcripts of Vivekananda's lectures, which occupy about 2,000 pages, or 40% of the material. His writings occupy 13% of the works and his letters 20%. Amazingly, nearly 20% of the works are written not by Vivekananda but by others; these include the notes of his class talks and conversations. Nearly 300 pages, or 6% of the material, are actually newspaper clippings of his lectures and interviews reported in the media. We can be certain about the accuracy of the lecture-transcripts, since most of them were taken down by J. J. Goodwin, an expert stenographer whose efficiency and skill were acknowledged by Vivekananda himself.[1] While the accuracy of Vivekananda's writings and letters is beyond doubt, the same cannot be said about the media reports and the notes others took of his class talks, interviews and conversations. Their accuracy can be affirmed only to the extent that they are in harmony with the ideas presented in his lectures and writings.

All in all, the *Complete Works* are a mixed bag. They are filled with ideas, an overwhelming abundance of them, but these ideas are scattered all over the nine volumes, and come from sources of variable accuracy. Moreover, the core of Vivekananda's thought is gleaned from the lectures he gave to different audiences at different times in America, Europe and India. All of his lectures were extempore. Their contexts were different, the times were different, and the audiences were different. Given the circumstances, a systematically organized presentation of ideas is not what one looks for in the *Complete Works*. They are not a *book* that Vivekananda wrote. They are a *compilation*. Had Vivekananda written a book, it would have been far easier to study and understand his philosophy of life. But his time was short. He wrote no books.[2] This has presented no small difficulty to serious students of his life and works.

The only instance when we are able to get a reasonably good idea of Vivekananda's thoughts on a specific subject is when he gave a series of lectures or class talks on a focused theme to more or less the same audience. The most significant among these were the series he gave on the yogas, all of which were later compiled into successful books and also included in the *Complete Works*.[3] These are among the most widely read books in Vivekananda literature. He spoke of these as the "text-books" which would be the basis of work after his passing.[4] These books are also among the most inspiring to serious spiritual seekers, for the emphasis in them is on practice. As authentic and honest transcripts of his class talks, their value is inestimable. They encourage the reader to not only *understand* the path but also to *practice* it.

Both understanding and practice require a deeper engagement than merely reading of those texts. We wonder what Vivekananda said to his students before he gave the formal class, what he said to them afterward, what personal instructions he gave them, what questions they asked him and what his answers were—but we are completely in the dark on all of this, except for occasional hints which we get from other books containing reminiscences of his friends and students.[5]

Once again we wish Vivekananda had *written* a book. If wishes were horses, they would take us galloping back in time to be in Vivekananda's presence when he gave the teaching! But our wishes are not horses and, even if they were, time travel still belongs to science fiction. One solution is to find a competent teacher, as many have done since Vivekananda's passing, and learn the method systematically in order to begin the practice. Another solution is to find a dependable text and learn from it. No text can substitute for a living teacher, but it can at least help us begin our study and practice as best we can.

Such secondary texts are not new in religious literature. In Vedanta, for instance, the tradition holds that there are three primary texts (*prasthāna-traya*), namely, the Upaniṣads, the *Bhagavad Gītā*, and the *Brahma-Sūtras*. What has made these primary texts accessible, intelligible, and eminently practicable is a plethora of secondary texts comprising commentaries (*bhāṣya*), critiques (*vārtika*), and explanatory notes (*tikā*) on the primary texts. Such commentarial literature, prevalent in all religions, elaborates on what may be terse, supplements what may seem insufficient, modifies what may need revision, and applies the wisdom to the changing realities of social life and to the unchanging truth that lies within.

Vivekananda's teachings are a commentary on Vedanta, not unlike the commentaries of the great ācāryas of the past but in a style and format more suited to our present needs. Take the case of Śaṅkarācārya's commentaries: those that came after him annotated his work by writing supplementary commentaries, critiques and explanatory notes, responding to questions, doubts, and criticisms of others, especially of competing schools of thought. This dialectic resulted in a philosophically robust and spiritually rich tradition that continues to nourish the lives of truth seekers to this day. A similar phenomenon is yet to occur in a serious way with regard to Vivekananda literature.[6] There is a real need for commentaries, critiques and explanatory notes on Vivekananda's teachings and this book dares to take the first small step in that direction.

Vivekananda's class talks on karma yoga were given in New York in the months of December 1895 and January 1896—four classes for beginners and four for advanced students. His book *Karma Yoga* (included in the first volume of his *Complete Works*) comprises the transcripts of these eight class talks.[7] But insights that are a part of karma yoga can be found in the rest of his literature as well. In this book I have made an effort to bring together his insights related to the study and practice of karma yoga and, in so doing, express my understanding of Vivekananda's approach to the subject. The book can be read as a commentary on his teachings on karma yoga, but it is not intended to replace the original class talks. It is not the purpose of commentaries to be surrogates.

Besides, nothing can substitute for the life-transforming power of Vivekananda's words. The endnotes in this book, therefore, point to those glowing words in order to encourage the reader to make an independent study of the original books. I hope that in the course of time such independent studies will produce more commentaries and critiques, initiating new lines of thought and deepening our understanding of Vivekananda. Besides providing in the endnotes extensive quotes from Vivekananda's *Complete Works* (CW) on which this commentary is based, I have also moved to the endnotes additional information and remarks in order to retain the focus of the commentary on the essentials of karma yoga study and practice.

The structure of this book is simple. The introductory chapter explores the meaning and scope of yoga. It also examines Vivekananda's classification of yoga into four categories, showing how it cuts across religious boundaries and provides a genuinely universal way to understand spiritual disciplines. The second chapter examines the elements of the karma theory essential to understanding the method of karma yoga. Each of Vivekananda's four yogas has a "key" with which to unlock its potential. The key to karma yoga is detachment, which is the focus of the third chapter.

While the first three chapters deal with *understanding* karma yoga, the fourth chapter is about the karma yoga *practice.* Right understanding is essential for right practice. We cannot put something to practical use until we know clearly what that something is. Conceptual clarity often paves the way to optimal practice. The fourth chapter is an attempted answer to the question: "I am fascinated by karma yoga and want to practice it. How do I go about it?" My hope is that serious students of karma yoga will find at least something in this book to get them started on a systematic daily practice. After all, as Vivekananda wrote in a letter: "There are books by the million. Oh, for an ounce of practice!"[8]

Even a little practice will yield results that will encourage the student to walk the walk to freedom with greater faith, hope and enthusiasm. That is what the fifth and final chapter is about: results. Just as the value of a tree is judged by the quality of its fruits, the value of a practice is judged by the quality of its results. What kinds of results are expected from a karma yoga practice? What are the guideposts and what is the final destination?

We return to the question that brought us to the study and practice of karma yoga. What can it do for me? The answer to this question *before* we begin the practice may be tentative and speculative. Not so *after* the practice is begun: our answer then will be more confident and more real. After all, the fruit in one's mouth is more real and more tasty than the idea of the fruit in one's mind.

With deepest gratitude and humility I dedicate this book to the first karma yogi I met in my life—my mother. Remembering a little book of Vivekananda that she placed in the hands of her ten-year-old son, I now place *this* little book in her hands.

ONE

Yoga

———

*I*t is simple to be happy, but it is difficult to be simple. Odd as it may sound, it is easy to be complicated. We have already accomplished that feat with remarkable ease. A simple, unicellular organism has over time evolved into an alarmingly complex creature, which is what each of us is today. The complexity within us extends from our bodies to our minds and intellects, engulfing our capacity to feel, to think, and to work. All of this has changed us into complicated beings who are, paradoxically enough, doomed to a humdrum existence.

On the face of it, our lives may seem anything but humdrum. After all, there is *so* much going on around us and in our personal lives that "humdrum" seems an unfair description. But if we step back and take an honest even if unsentimental look, it is difficult not to notice the monotony which pervades our lives. We rejoice, we grieve, we celebrate, we mourn, we eat, we work, we sleep, we laugh, we cry—what are our lives other than a bunch of these and similar activities? One human life is not essen-

1

tially different from another. It is the same jumble of activities: the details vary but not much else. The basic template of every life is boringly identical: birth, growth, change, decay and death.[1] As the end draws near, we feel stressed, exhausted, spent, and have to wait with trepidation and anxiety until death relieves us of the recurring pain and the persistent monotony. If this seems like a decidedly unpoetic and dreary picture of our lives, it is because no poetry or optimism can effectively mask the existential imperfection, mortality, and bondage inherent in our human experience.

The good news is that this is not the whole story. Not all clouds are dark and every cloud has a silver lining. We are no longer simple, it is true, but it is possible for us to abandon our complexity and return to our native simplicity. It is possible for us to shed our imperfection and regain our lost perfection. Indeed, it is possible for us to become pure, free and immortal—again. For that is what we were before we found ourselves in the present situation.

There are different explanations for how and why things changed. These explanations are enshrined in a variety of worldviews presented in the language of religion, philosophy, psychology or science. The religious explanations are often allegorical and have become a part of mythology but not, on that account, less worthy of careful scrutiny. Whatever be the explanation for a "fall" from the state of simplicity—often portrayed as departure from the state of perfection and grace—the process that takes us back to our original simplicity is called yoga. In Vedanta, the return to the state of perfection and grace is simply known as returning to our *own nature.*

Yoga as a process must be distinguished from the school of Indian philosophy which is also known as Yoga. There are six orthodox schools of Indian philosophy: they are called "orthodox" because they acknowledge the Vedas as a revealed scripture and trace their insights to the wisdom found in the Vedas. The six schools are: Pūrva Mīmāṁsā, Uttara Mīmaṁsā (better known as Vedānta), Sāṁkhya, Yoga, Nyāya, and Vaiśeṣika. In this book, yoga as a school of philosophy will be referred to as Yoga (with a capital "y"), and yoga as a process will be yoga (with a lowercase "y"). As a process, yoga finds a place in all these six schools of philosophy.[2]

The Word "Yoga"

The meaning of a word changes over time. Sometimes the change is huge, often it is minimal. When a word enters the mainstream of a different culture and language, the problem acquires an added layer of complexity. The history of the word "yoga" is no exception to this. To go back to what the word meant originally, we need to look at its Sanskrit roots.

The word "yoga" is traced to two different roots by the Sanskrit grammarian Pāṇini and hence has two distinct meanings. Its first meaning is "concentration" (*yuj samādhau*) and it is in this sense that the word is used by Patañjali in his Yoga aphorisms. The second meaning of yoga is "union" (*yujir yoge*), and it is in this sense that the word is mostly used in Vedanta and other traditions. The various systems of yoga trace the word's meaning to either of these two roots. Sometimes the connection to the root-meanings is direct and obvious, and sometimes it is not.

The two meanings complement each other, especially for those who see yoga primarily as "union." In Vedanta, yoga represents the union between the individual self (*jīvātman*) and the supreme self (*paramātman*), and to achieve this union—no matter what specific method is followed—concentration is absolutely essential. In the dualistic schools of Indian philosophy, such as Sāṁkhya and Yoga, reality is divided into the principle of consciousness (*puruṣa*) and the principle of materiality (*prakṛti*). The *puruṣa* is said to be trapped in the snares of *prakṛti*, so the two are already sort of united. The goal, therefore, is not union but separation of the *puruṣa* from the *prakṛti*—and these schools of thought employ the word "yoga" as concentration. But what is concentration other than uniting the mind with the object it is concentrating on? The *puruṣa* achieves union with itself when it concentrates on its own nature as distinct from *prakṛti*. So in a roundabout way, "yoga" as union also finds an echo in these schools of thought.

With the burgeoning popularity of yoga all over the world, the word has now entered mainstream English and other major languages. Plucked from its historical, linguistic, and traditional origins, yoga has taken diverse forms and acquired a host of qualifiers to distinguish one variety from another. Sometimes a type of yoga may distinguish itself naturally by its specialized focus, new insights, and unique practices. Just as often, the commodification of yoga and its marketing in modern times have made it necessary for some teachers to highlight their variety of yoga as "different" in order to survive in the competitive field. Nevertheless, in one form or another, yoga as union and yoga as concentration still endure in all of the multifarious ways in which yoga is understood and practiced all over the world.

The Yoga Tree

The roots of the yoga tree are traced to the Vedas, although there is a view that they might even be pre-Vedic. In the northwestern part of the Indian subcontinent, archeological finds have revealed a sophisticated civilization in the Indus valley, which is believed to be as old as 3000 BCE. The excavations in the Indus valley sites have led to the discovery of seals with representations of figures seated in yogic postures, the most famous of which "is seated with arms extended and resting on the knees in a classical meditative posture."[3]

From these Vedic or pre-Vedic origins, yoga as a discipline evolved in different ways. While each way has its own distinct identity, each is also porous enough to make cross-connections with other yoga systems. With a long history of borrowing from others and supplementing one another, the different systems of yoga look like the intertwined branches of a tree. Separating these branches or identifying them is by no means easy. While doing this is not an essential exercise, it is nevertheless rewarding, for it at least gives us an idea of how huge the tree is and how complex its branches are. There is no universally accepted version of the yoga tree, so how we envision the branches depends on our creative categorization skills.

One simple way is to categorize yoga based on the *textual sources*. Every major text which has significant references to yoga can be considered a branch of the yoga tree. We find references to yoga in the Vedas (particularly in the Upaniṣads),[4] in the epics such as the *Rāmāyaṇa* and the *Mahābhārata* (particularly in the *Gītā*),[5] in the Purāṇas and the different Smṛtis.[6] We find references also in the texts associated with the Vaiṣṇavas, the Śaivas, and the Śāktas, and the lives and teachings of the saints and teachers in those traditions. There are references to yoga in *Carakasaṁhitā*,[7] *Viśudhimāgga* of Buddhaghoṣa and in *Yogadṛṣṭisamuccaya* of the eighth-century Jain author Haribhadra.

The ubiquitousness of "yoga" in so many texts that originated at different times in different parts of the Indian subcontinent is amazing. The various ways in which the word "yoga" is understood and the variety of practices which are identified as yoga in these texts are mind-boggling. While this shows us how vast the field is, it is almost impossible to get a bird's-eye view of yoga by looking at these innumerable textual sources. It quickly becomes apparent that the categorization on the basis of textual sources is simple but not particularly useful.

A useful way to conceive the branches of the yoga tree is by focusing on some of the major *spiritual traditions,* each with its own worldview and a theology that accords a prominent role to yoga. At least four major traditions spring to mind: Pātañjala, Haṭha, Vedāntic, and Tāntric. As the name indicates, the Pātañjala branch is developed in the Yoga school of philosophy systematized by Patañjali and it uses the term yoga to mean concentration. Its aim is separation of the *puruṣa* from *prakṛti* and the meditation practice in it is called *dhyāna.* In Patañjali's *Yoga-Sūtras,* we find a harmonious blending of two other subsidiary branches called *kriyā* yoga and *aṣṭāṅga* yoga.

The second branch of the yoga tree is Haṭha, often wrongly (and sometimes pejoratively) identified with mere bodily postures. The name Haṭha is a combination of *ha* and *sa* (*tha*), where *ha* stands for the sun nerve-current (*īḍā*) and *sa* stands for the moon nerve-current (*piṅgalā*). The goal of Haṭha is to bring about the retention and union (*yoga*) of vital forces (*prāṇa*) flowing through these nerve currents. This is done through muscular contractions called seals (*mudra*) and locks (*bandha*), which unite the vital forces within the central nerve-current (*suṣumnā*). The heat produced by this union arouses the supremely refined and potent force known as *kuṇḍalinī*, which is symbolically represented as a coiled serpent. The *kuṇḍalinī* rises through the central nerve current, piercing and opening several centers of consciousness (*cakra*) and eventually reaching the thousand-petaled center (*sahasrāra*) at the crown of the head, resulting in the highest samādhi.[8]

Vedantic yoga is based on the idea of yoga as union and the meditation practice in it is called *upāsanā*. In Vedanta the goal is to join the individual self with the supreme self. The "joining" is only apparent because the "separation" is also apparent. Even though apparent, it feels real due to ignorance. The self (*ātman*), who is one and indivisible, apparently gets divided, hence its division into an individual self and the supreme self. These qualifiers—"individual" and "supreme"—drop off and the self alone remains when, through practices that involve the training of the various functions of the mind, knowledge dawns and ignorance disappears.

Developed in the Tantra schools in the Śaiva, Śākta, Vaiṣṇava and also Buddhist traditions, Tantric yoga has several branches among which are *mantra* yoga and *laya* yoga. The *kuṇḍalinī* plays a significant role in Tantric systems and the practice of mantra repetition (*japa*) is highly developed. Based on yoga as union, the goal of Tantric yoga is to unite the individual self (represented by the *kuṇḍalinī*) with the supreme self. Haṭha yoga and Tāntric yoga are sometimes jointly called *kuṇḍalinī* yoga.

There are also secondary and tertiary branches, which have grown out of these major traditions and added to the complexity and richness of the yoga tree. For instance, there are versions of yoga found in Tibetan Buddhism and in the Yogācāra school (also known as Vijñānavāda) of Mahāyāna Buddhism. Jainism also has its own versions in the Digambara sect and the Śvetāmbara Terāpanthī sect.

Visualizing the tree in terms of the various spiritual traditions is thus a useful way to understand the scope and extent of yoga. This form of categorization, however, depends on a tradition's use of the word "yoga," and so it can survey only the traditions that originated in the Indian subcontinent or the recent New Age traditions that have mushroomed in other parts of the world. What if a tradition has practices that clearly are a form of yoga but are not called by that name? If a categorization can embrace even such traditions, then *that* would be not only useful but also universal.

Vivekananda's Four Yogas

It was Swami Vivekananda's genius that offered a universal way of categorizing yoga, and he did it by sifting the various practices on the basis of the various functions of the mind.[9] I am using the word "mind" here in a generic sense, referring to the invisible part of our personality that (1) governs our emotions, thoughts, hopes and fears, (2) responds to external situations, and (3) acts as the subtle engine that powers and moves the body. Understood thus, we see that it is the mind which raises questions, seeks answers, creates meaning, and chooses the practice. When the mind is strong, healthy and clear, it raises the right questions, recognizes the right answer, creates the right meaning, and chooses the right practice. When the mind is weak, sick and confused, it does just the opposite. Little wonder, then, that it is the mind that needs careful nurturing and attention. No matter which spiritual tradition becomes our home, it is primarily the mind which connects us to it.

When we listen with attention to what the mind does, we are able to distinguish its various functions. The mind is the receptacle of a powerful force called emotion, which influences a major part of our lives, perhaps more than many of us realize. Most of the decisions we take and the choices we make in life are guided more by our feelings than reason. We often decide something emotionally and then reason our way to the decision, but our mind tampers with the chronology and makes us feel that we *first* used reason to think it through and *then* made the choice we feel comfortable with. When the mind is in its "feeling" mode, it is called by the same name, mind (*manas*), or sometimes "heart."[10] When the mind is in its "reasoning" mode, it is called intellect (*buddhi*).

Besides feeling and reasoning, the mind performs another vital function: willing. In many ways, it is the will that connects the mind with the body. The will is the link between what happens in the invisible world of the mind and the visible world of the body. It is only when the will (*icchā*) gives its nod of approval that a desire (*vāsanā*) of the heart becomes an intention (*saṁkalpa*) and is transformed into action (*karma*).

Vivekananda's pure and luminous mind cut through the layers of name and form enveloping the various spiritual practices not only in Hinduism, the tradition he was raised in, but in other religions as well. What he discovered beneath the dazzling variety of spiritual disciplines and practices was the human mind operating in its various modes. While emotion played a major role in some practices, reasoning did in others, and the will was predominant in yet others. It was based on these primary functions of the human mind—the affective function of the heart, the cognitive function of the intellect, and the conative function of the will—that Vivekananda offered his own categories of yoga and showed how four primary groupings could encompass all spiritual practices cutting across religious boundaries.

To the practices in which emotions play a major role he gave the name bhakti yoga. Those in which reasoning is the primary practice were given the name jñāna yoga. The practices in which the will is dominant were recognized by him as either rāja yoga or karma yoga.[11] In rāja yoga, the will is primarily directed *inward*, studying, analyzing, and controlling the powers of the mind. In karma yoga, the will is primarily directed *outward*, studying, analyzing and controlling our engagement with the world through work.

All spiritual disciplines, no matter in which religious tradition they are rooted and no matter who practices them, can thus be categorized in one of these four yogas. The human mind and its primary functions, after all, are universal. The four-yogas model thus is not only practical and useful but also all-embracing. In the midst of religious diversity, it finds a connecting link which affirms unity, even as it preserves the distinctive character of each practice without diminishing it. Nor is the word "yoga" itself so important as to be non-negotiable. The four yogas can be called by other names, or by no name at all, and they would still be equally meaningful and useful. "What's in a

name? that which we call a rose / By any other name
would smell as sweet."

Harmony of Yogas

While it is easy to separate the functions of the mind on
paper and study them independently, in practice the mind
acts as one unit; it is impossible to isolate and employ any
specific function to the exclusion of others. In other words,
even when emotions are uppermost in the mind, reasoning
and will are never totally absent. No one function of the
mind can muscle out the others completely. We can only
speak about a function of the mind being predominant at
any given time, recognizing that the other functions play
subsidiary roles during that period.[12] While it is not impossible to have all of the functions equally developed in a
person's mental makeup, in most people we generally see
one function more developed than others.

Which yoga appeals to a person and which practice may
be most effective depends on the predominant trait of the
person's mind. Thus some are spontaneously drawn to
bhakti yoga while others are drawn to jñāna yoga, and so
on. It is good to keep in mind that bhakti yoga, for
instance, may deal primarily with emotions, but that does
not mean that it is totally bereft of reasoning and will. It
only means that bhakti yoga practices are woven around
the affective function of the heart. There is plenty of
opportunity to apply one's reason and exercise one's will in
bhakti yoga. The same principle applies to the other yogas
as well.

None of these four yogas is easy and none is difficult. If a
person has both interest in a particular yoga and fitness for
its practice, then that yoga would be "easy" for the person

and the other yogas might seem "difficult," even incomprehensible. No matter which yoga ends up being our favored path to freedom, the need for the three P's—purity, patience and perseverance—can never be overestimated. These were the three P's that Swami Vivekananda repeatedly invoked in his letters and teachings to his disciples.[13] With the three P's the practice of yoga becomes joyful and fulfilling. Without the three P's, it quickly degenerates into a sham.

Not only are these yogas equally easy or difficult but they are also equally effective. Their ultimate goal is the same: to manifest our true nature, which is divine, pure and perfect.[14] Every yoga can take its practitioner to this goal.[15] Sri Ramakrishna's words, "As many faiths, so many paths," can also be employed to affirm the harmony of the four yogas: "As many yogas, so many paths." It is we who choose the path, or so it seems until we discover that it is the path that chooses us. Given our mental disposition and interest, we don't quite choose a specific yoga but are drawn to it instinctively, often irresistibly, making us wonder whether it was perhaps the yoga that was attracting us toward itself and we responded to it like a piece of iron to a magnet.

Synthesis of Yogas

While each yoga is capable on its own of taking its practitioner to the goal, the spiritual discipline of some may include more than one yoga, depending on their interests and mental makeup. Considering that each of these four yogas allows for a fuller expression of a specific function of the mind, it would seem even necessary to find a place for all the yogas in one's daily practice in order to develop all the functions to the fullest extent possible. Can this be done? Absolutely. Not only do the yogas not conflict with one another but, on the contrary, they supplement one another.

A combination of yogas helps eliminate some of the possible pitfalls in the practice of a single yoga. For instance, if jñāna yoga is practiced haphazardly, there is a real danger that it may end up being nothing more than dry intellectualism, a far cry from a path to freedom that it is meant to be. But when combined with bhakti yoga practices, that danger is minimized. Similarly, an exclusive pursuit of bhakti yoga, if done in a slipshod way, may become nothing more than weepy sentimentalism. This can be kept under control by combining it with practices employing reasoning and will in the other three yogas. Since everyone does some work or other, it is essential for karma yoga to be an inevitable part of any practice, no matter which yoga provides the primary focus. Thus it makes good sense to have a wholesome personal practice which includes elements of all yogas. Not all yogas may be equally present in a composite practice. One (or more) among them may still be more prominent than others and that is to be expected. What kind of combination would be ideal is best determined with the help of one's spiritual teacher (*guru*).[16]

It is vital that disparate practices from different yogas are not thrown together randomly like clothes in a laundry bag. The synthesis of yogas is more than just doing a little bit of every yoga in the course of a day. Any spiritual practice must be organically whole, meaning every part of it must be integrated with others and all must together reinforce one another. A wholesome spiritual practice is not unlike an ideal, healthy meal in which every item, though distinct, is in harmony with others and together they supplement one another, providing the right amount of nourishment.

The best way to accomplish this is to cultivate one-pointed-ness, the capacity to zero in on the work in hand. What we need is both an intense capacity to attach our mind to the current activity and, once that activity is over, an intense detachment to leave it and take up the next activity. We need to practice every yoga with total concentration as if our entire life depended on it or as if it alone would lead us to spiritual freedom. Once a practice associated with that yoga is over, we need to detach ourselves from it and redirect our focus on the practice of another yoga, throwing ourselves as fully into it as we did in the earlier one.[17] This will bring about both a harmonious develop-ment of our mind and also a natural way to synthesize the elements of different yogas in our spiritual practice.[18]

The short introduction to "yoga" in this chapter has hope-fully shed some light on a term that has gained currency in many parts of the world and, perhaps for that reason, is understood (and misunderstood) in forms that can be bewildering. We have seen what the literal meaning of yoga is, where its roots lie, and in how many ways we can classify its different forms. Vivekananda's formulation of the four yogas based on the different functions of the human mind, the importance of harmony of yogas, and the possibility of their synthesis have also been discussed. Now it's time to turn to "karma," the other keyword in our study of karma yoga.

TWO

Karma

*I*t is helpful to begin by revisiting the word "karma" and see what it really means. Karma—like "yoga"—has now entered mainstream English. It is invoked in diverse situations and has acquired a range of meanings. Recently in Boston I saw a car ahead of me with a bumper-sticker proclaiming, "Good karma is cost effective." A friend reported seeing another that said, "My karma ran over your dogma." Such funny, enigmatic, cryptic quotes often point to some aspect related to karma but, just as often, they also produce bizarre and question-able ideas regarding karma.

In order to recover the word "karma" from its accretions we need to go back and take another look at what it origi-nally meant and what the karma theory (*karmavāda*) is all about.

The Karma Theory

Derived from Sanskrit *kṛ* ("to do"), karma simply means work or action.[1] Every work we do, physical or mental, is karma.[2] Some of our work is involuntary. Most physiological processes—like the pumping action of the heart, the function of the kidneys, or the digestive process—are involuntary and occur without any conscious effort. But a lot of other things are done voluntarily and with conscious effort. It is these latter set of actions that are of special interest in the karma theory. If work is *karma,* the results of work are *karma-phala* (lit. "the fruits of work"). In popular usage, though, even the results of work are referred to as karma, and that is one reason why matters related to karma become confusing and are sometimes misunderstood.

The karma theory is, of course, a "theory," meaning that it cannot be objectively proved, although it provides a logical explanation for the way things are. But before we come to what makes it a "theory" and not "truth," we can see that its basic assumptions are difficult to deny because they are either a part of our daily experience or they lie at the heart of our hope for this world.

First, it is difficult to deny that actions have consequences. Secondly, it is difficult to deny that we want our lives to be happy, meaningful and fulfilling. Thirdly, our hope for justice makes it difficult to deny that goodness will lead to happy results and wickedness to unhappy consequences. Put together, that's the essence of the karma theory. We reap what we sow. There is no need to blame anyone for our sorrow or be indebted to anyone for our happiness. Everything is earned. Nothing comes gratis. We are responsible both for our actions and for their results.[3]

While karma can be of many different kinds, the results of karma—in terms of experience—are primarily of two kinds: happiness (*sukha*) or sorrow (*duḥkha*). When a work is successful or meaningful in some way, it brings happiness. Its opposite brings sorrow. Happiness and sorrow are the two basic experiential results of work, although their duration, expression and intensity may vary. Sometimes we can trace a result to its cause, but often we cannot. When we cannot, it doesn't mean that the cause does not exist. It simply means that we don't know what the cause is. No one knows for sure which karma would produce what specific result, except in generic, experiential terms. "Inscrutable are the ways of karma," as the *Gītā* (4.17) points out.

It is important to remember that karma determines only our *experience*, not our *actions*. This is either not known or is often forgotten by many, and yet understanding this well is the key to *not* misunderstanding the role of karma in our lives. For this reason I am going to repeat it: *karma determines only our experience, not our actions*. Our present happiness or sorrow is the result of our past karma, but what we *do* now is not the result of past karma. While no one can change the past, we have all the freedom in the world to choose our present actions. It is wrong to hold past karma responsible for our foolish choices or muddle-headed decisions of the present. A lot of the misunderstanding about karma occurs because this distinction between *experience* and *action* is ignored.

Why do we need the karma theory? We don't really need the karma theory per se. What most people seem to need is a credible explanation for the way things are. Some people may not care or may be too busy with more immediate concerns, but others want to know whether our existence is governed by any rule or stuff just happens randomly. Such a question seems inevitable when we see the discrepancies that are found all around us, and especially if we are at the receiving end. Looking at our own lives, we may be at a loss to understand what we did to deserve some of the pain and suffering. Looking out at the world raises questions too: we find that some people are happy, some are not; some attain easy success, some fail in spite of herculean effort; some are born and raised in a favorable environment, some others in extremely difficult ones; some die young, some live long. What determines such varied outcomes? How can we explain all this?

Several answers have been offered. One answer is that it's all a matter of luck. There is no logic in life. Life is determined by chance. What this answer means is that we really don't know why things are the way they are.

Another answer involves God. We are told that everything happens by the will of God. God determines who should be happy and who should be miserable, who should be successful and who should fail, who should live long and who should die young. We can neither predict nor understand the divine will, so it's no use trying. All that we can do is submit to it with faith and without questioning. If this were true, then it would be difficult to believe that God loves us all equally. It looks like God has favorites and there are folks whom God just doesn't like. Which brings into question God's uniqueness. It makes God not too different from you and me. Such a God cannot command our unreserved love and surrender. If there is no justifiable reason why God would make one person happy and condemn another to suffer, then we are dealing with a whimsical God. This kind of God is of no use to us. Better to "throw him overboard into the Pacific Ocean!"[4] as Vivekananda once exclaimed.

In order to absolve God of any seeming injustice, we are sometimes told that those who suffer now for God will rejoice later in heaven. Much can be said about this kind of thinking, but it is enough to point out the obvious: this is a diabolical way of serving justice.[5] More importantly, it does not answer the question why people should suffer here at all. Clearly, involving God in the affairs of the world and yet preserving God's neutrality and wisdom is a task filled with contradictions. If it is claimed that God does not distribute joy and sorrow arbitrarily, then it brings us squarely back to the idea of karma.

The karma theory does not believe in chance and it keeps God out of its explanation.[6] It bluntly tells us that we are "the creators of our own destiny."[7] Our present experience is determined by our past actions. Our future experience will be determined by what we do here and now. We shape our own future.

Taking Control of One's Life

This understanding of karma restores life back into our hands. We rarely question the presence of happiness in our lives. That's usually taken for granted. It's something we feel we are entitled to. What we don't want is pain and the sorrow that accompanies it. A life filled with happiness with no trace of pain and sorrow is most people's dream. That is the kind of life promised in heaven by religions of the world. But life as we know it here and now is different: it has both happiness and sorrow, and we simply cannot have one without the other.[8]

Yet when pain and sorrow crush our hearts, we don't stop questioning: "Why *me*? Who is responsible for this?" The general tendency is to find an external cause which can be blamed for our woes. This may help a little, for it seems to free us from the responsibility for our suffering—but it does nothing really to solve the problem.[9]

On a deeper level, it in fact exacerbates the problem. If there are forces out in the world which control when I should be happy and when I should be miserable, then that makes me only a puppet. What happened to my much boasted freedom? If anything can happen to anyone at anytime for no good reason, why should I be good or do good? Why should I not cheat and lie my way to pleasure and enjoyment? This leaves in tatters the whole fabric of meaningful social life, besides making ethics and morality irrelevant.

Freedom and responsibility go hand in hand. If we want to be free, we need to take responsibility. Karma gives it to us, and that is why it is most empowering. It allows us control over our own lives. We don't have to depend on luck or fate. We don't have to grovel in dust before a whimsical God who dispenses favors to the chosen few and casts the rest into eternal damnation. No one but us should have that kind of control over our lives. Karma gives us that control. We can make or break our own future. If we learn from the past and apply that wisdom to our actions in the present, we are assured of a brighter future.[10] Karma also makes ethical and moral life meaningful and important.

Viewing life through the karma lens helps us grow into mature adults and leave behind our childish traits. For instance, we realize how foolish it is to blame others when things go wrong for us. Life is a mixed bag: there are ups and there are downs. We just need to ride the wave. Suffering is a part of life but being miserable is optional. It makes little sense to be miserable when, just as easily, we can face the difficult situation with a positive frame of mind, no matter how arduous the struggle. It is true that suffering is no fun and can make life difficult, but why should that make us miserable by default? No one can make us miserable but us.[11] Nothing can happen to us unless we allow it to do so.[12] Karma teaches us to look at everything from the subjective standpoint.[13]

The benefits of understanding life in terms of karma are clear and immediate, but karma is still a "theory" because it cannot be objectively proved, although it provides a reasonable explanation for why things are the way they are. It is good to keep in mind, however, that the alternative answers that are offered—everything a matter of chance or a result of God's will—are theories as well.[14] Whether karma *really* exists no one knows and no one can prove or disprove. But that doesn't matter in the least. What does matter—and what experience has proved to be true—is that *understanding* life in terms of karma satisfies both the head and the heart. It invests life with meaning and empowers the person to face life boldly.

Everyone is, of course, free to accept whichever theory makes the best sense to them. The karma theory is not touted as the only explanation, nor even the best explanation. People are different and one theory cannot satisfy everyone. The advantage of the karma theory is that it is logical. It finds the solution within the system, instead of depending on an extraneous factor such as chance or an extra-cosmic God.[15] Moreover, unlike the alternative theories, it views individual life on a much larger canvas—not limiting it to a truncated version that is compressed to a period sandwiched between birth and death.

Karma and Reincarnation

Most religious—and even some nonreligious—traditions accept that we reap what we sow. When goodness is sowed, a good plant sprouts with flowers that bring joy and fulfillment. When wickedness is sowed, a poisonous plant sprouts producing unpleasant consequences. This simple law of life provides an incentive to moral life and makes it meaningful. The incentive to religious life comes mostly from concerns related to death and what happens after it. This often gets mythologized through descriptions of the joys of heaven and the suffering in hell. Just as often, though, the incentive to religious life can also come through the relentless quest to transcend one's limitations[16] and recognizing that a good and disciplined way of life is the only way to fulfill that quest. Something similar to karma thus is already playing a significant role in moral living and in the worldviews that most religions present. The karma theory, however, applies not just to what happens *after* birth but also to what happened *before* birth.

What, if anything, happened before birth? How could we do anything before we were born? Did we exist before we were born? Now we are entering a territory which is primarily governed by faith and scriptural testimony. Let me just state here what Vedanta's answer is: Put simply, we did exist before we were born. There never was a time when we didn't exist.[17] Each of us is the Ātman. We are one with existence (*sat*). Our true nature is pure consciousness (*cit*). We are infinite (*ananta*) and hence naturally blissful (*ānanda*).[18] Such as we are, "birth" simply means acquiring a body and "death" means separation from the body. The bodies come and go, we don't. We always are. We exist eternally. The body is a part of this material world. It is "dust"—which temporarily becomes animated and looks conscious as long as it is filled with life (*prāṇa*) and consciousness (*cit* or *caitanya*). When life and consciousness depart, the dust returns to dust.[19]

Where were we before our birth? We dwelt within other material coverings—different bodies, equally "dusty"—and lived somewhere in this seemingly infinite universe. We have no idea how big this universe is. This tiny little planet called the Earth in a nondescript solar system powered by a minor star called the Sun in one among God-knows-how-many galaxies may not be the only place where life is possible. Or it may be the only such place. Who knows and who really cares? Questions are being raised about the possibility of more universes in addition to the one universe that we know about. There are so many questions and, alas, so few answers.

Even our conception of more than one universe is limited: after all, we can only conceive of what our limited mind can help us conceptualize, which it does based on the sensory input of the equally limited senses. What about the reality that is beyond the reach of the senses? All heavens and hells that we find in various religions occupy spaces that are not accessed by our human senses, although they are conceived by the mind. We cannot, of course, imagine what is beyond our imagination. In short, it's beyond us to gauge the extent of whatever is out there.

It is "there," in gross or subtle spaces, that we are "born" and we "die"— meaning, each of us acquires a body and then becomes separated from it. This has happened many,

many times in the past—and can happen any number of times in the future. There is no end. A circle has no beginning and no end. We just go round and round in a circle. Everything around us keeps changing all the time. There is continuous movement. The Sanskrit word for this continually changing experience is *saṁsāra* and, because the movement is in a circle (*cakra*), it is called "the circle of relative existence" (*saṁsāra-cakra*).[20]

What's the point of all this? Frankly, there is no point at all.[21] No one knows why we go round in circles. No one knows whether this is only our imagination or it is something that we *really* do. Either way, our present experience of mortality and lack of total fulfillment is undeniable. Let's face it: we may have our *beliefs*, but we have no *knowledge* of where we were before our birth and where we will be after our death. Birth and death are a mystery. The process that solves the mystery through the power of the intellect is jñāna yoga. The process that solves it using the power of emotion is bhakti yoga. The process that solves it by applying the power of the will to one's mind and its processes is rāja yoga. The process that solves it by applying the power of the will to work and its effects is karma yoga.

The goal is to solve the mystery, get out of the circle, and be free. What path we choose to follow and what it is named and who discovered it are secondary details that do not matter in the least. The house is on fire. We must get out of it as soon as we can. Our safe escape out of the burning house is more important than quibbling endlessly about the merits of the different escape routes.[22]

It is of little importance whether there *really* is reincarnation.[23] What matters is whether thinking about our life and our own selves in terms of karma and reincarnation helps us solve the mystery and be free. Intensely practical, karma yoga focuses on solving the problem of life and death, and on attaining lasting freedom and fulfillment. Generations of karma yogis have proved beyond doubt the power and effectiveness of karma yoga. Guiding their lives based on the insights found in the karma theory has helped people solve the mystery.

We don't need the boat after we have crossed the river and have no intention to return. We don't need the karma theory after we have gone beyond the domain of karma and the inevitable sorrow that fills it. Karma is a means, not an end in itself. The truth of karma lies in its effectiveness as a means to go beyond sorrow.

Karma and Sorrow

We experience both joy and sorrow in life. It is possible to see our lives as continually alternating between smiles and tears when we respond and react to different situations. Life seems to have place for both joy and sorrow. Yet some of the greatest minds have thought otherwise. Buddha, for instance, taught that life is suffering.[24] Earlier than him, Krishna said as much when he referred to the world as "joyless" and as "the abode of sorrow."[25] It is helpful to take these words to heart and ponder over them, for we know that they came from people who were not frustrated or depressed. They came from people who knew what they were talking about.

There are two kinds of sorrow: temporal and existential. Temporal sorrow is the sorrow that we experience in daily life and it alternates with temporal joy. That is what makes us feel that life is a mixture of both joy and sorrow. The joy derived from praise, recognition, success, and accomplishment is temporal in nature. So is the sorrow resulting from hunger, homelessness, poverty, betrayal, abuse, and cruelty. Both these kinds of joy and sorrow are time-bound and context-driven. Although affecting a significant segment of humanity, temporal sorrow is by no means universal, in the sense that not everyone is suffering on account of these. And even those who are suffering on account of these are not doing so at each and every moment.

The second kind of sorrow is existential, in the sense that it is connected with our very *existence* as human beings. No human being therefore is exempt from it. The suffering associated with the process of aging, illness and death is existential,[26] as is the suffering inherent in mental stress, anxiety and fear.[27] People are so preoccupied in dealing with temporal sorrow and in running after temporal joy that there is little time or interest in dealing with existential sorrow. In fact, most people don't even recognize it as such, even though they confront it all the time. A certain amount of sensitivity is needed to become aware of this deeper and subtler variety of sorrow. Aware or not, all human beings are subject to it—and it is referring to this all-pervasive sorrow that Krishna called the world "joyless" and Buddha saw it as filled with suffering.

Karma plays a role in both kinds of sorrow. Both temporal sorrow and temporal joy are a direct result of karma. Existential sorrow, on the other hand, results from a chain reaction in which karma plays a key role. Vedanta teachers often cite this chain to show why karma is a problem. We may call this chain a karma chain since it is karma that maintains it. Oddly enough, it is karma that can also snap it. Karma done in a right way—which is what karma yoga really is—breaks the chain, eliminates existential sorrow, and manifests existential joy and freedom.

If existential sorrow is the sorrow resulting from our very existence as human beings, existential joy is the joy that emanates from our very existence as the Ātman. This must be phrased more accurately, since we are always the Ātman whether we know it or not. Thus it would be more accurate to say: our *ignorance* of being the Ātman produces sorrow, and our *knowledge* of being the Ātman produces joy. Not surprisingly, the karma chain is produced by our ignorance, which makes us forget that we are divine, immortal and free. Our ignorance makes us feel that we are human, mortal and imperfect.

The Karma Chain

This is the karma chain: ignorance (*avidyā*) > desire (*kāma*) > action (*karma*) > birth (*janma*) > existential sorrow (*duhkha*). From this point forward, the chain becomes circular: karma > birth > sorrow > karma > birth > sorrow … and so it goes. This, as we have already seen, is the "circle of relative existence." An unconscious, instinctual, desire-propelled life keeps a person tied to the circle. A conscious life, guided by yoga, frees a person from the never-ending grind of the circular journey.

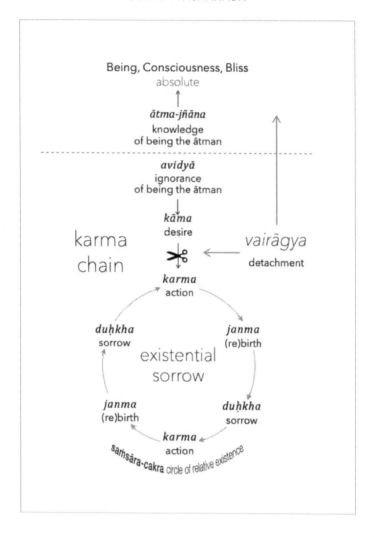

The chain apparently begins with ignorance. From where did this ignorance come? Why should there be any ignorance at all? How did we forget that we are the Ātman? An honest answer to these questions can only be, "I don't know."[28]

The same answer would apply even to the question: "When did this ignorance begin?" Every kind of ignorance seems as if it never had a beginning. For instance, since I don't know Japanese, it would seem that my ignorance of Japanese has always been with me. If I learn Japanese, this ignorance can end. According to Vedanta, the drama of the world, which includes you and me and everything else, begins with ignorance. What existed before that was only the infinite Being who is awareness itself. How extraordinary that awareness, or knowledge, now seems to be clouded by ignorance![29]

When the veil of ignorance covers the One, it seems as if oneness disappears and is replaced by the many. It seems as if the infinite disappears and is replaced by the finite. It seems as if wholeness disappears and is replaced by incompleteness. It is this sense of being incomplete that produces the desire to be complete. In order to fill the emptiness gnawing inside, the finite being desires all kinds of things that are outside. It is the power of the will that initiates action in order to fulfill those desires. Actions produce results: in experiential terms, the results take the form of joy and sorrow. But these can be experienced only through an instrument called the body. Hence the next step is the acquisition of a body through the process called birth, leading to life in the world. Filled with temporal and existential sorrow, the world provides plenty of it in the course of a lifetime.

But we don't just experience the results of past karma in life. We also *do* fresh karma, sowing the seeds for future experiences. Since the present life is too short to exhaust the experiences of all our past karma, another body is needed, and that is what leads to rebirth. And thus the chain becomes a circle and the finite being, now so ignorant as to have almost forgotten its true nature, revolves in this circle endlessly.

We are not talking about somebody else. That "finite being" is each one of us. This is the story of *our* lives. We reap the results of our past through the alternating experience of joy and sorrow. And, at the same time, we sow the seeds for the future by our present actions. We create the web of karma and its results, and we are hopelessly trapped in both. The only way to get out of the web is to cut it. The only way to snap the chain is to break one of its links. It is possible to do it and karma yoga shows us *how* to do it. The instrument that cuts the chain and breaks the vicious cycle is called detachment.

THREE

Detachment

---

*D*etachment is the ax which breaks the karma chain and snaps the link that connects desire with karma. We need to keep in mind that behind every link in the karma chain stands a conscious person. Thus, ignorance > desire > karma > birth > sorrow is not simply a chain that exists in a vacuum. It is a chain with which every one of us is intimately tied in a very personal way.

The pure, infinite and undivided consciousness—which is who you and I really are—was somehow veiled with ignorance and became forgetful of its infinitude. Now born as a finite being among other finite beings and objects, it desired to possess the objects and relate with people, which provided the motivation for karma. When karma in the form of physical or mental activity was done, it was time for the results to come in. Of what use is karma without its fruits? The fruits of karma arrived in the form of joy and sorrow, both of which were only manifestations of the underlying existential sorrow. More karma followed, resulting in more sorrow, the recurring process persisting to this day. The only way to end the vicious cycle is to break the chain.

The weakest link in the chain is the one that connects desire with karma. All the other links are fairly stable and largely beyond our control. How is the link that connects desire with karma broken? The process is simple and involves two kinds of detachment: detachment from desire and detachment from karma.

Detachment from Desire

Detachment from desire can occur in many ways. One way is to begin the process of detaching from material, world-centric desires by consciously cultivating spiritual, God-centric desires. This is done by purifying our emotions and directing them toward God. The desire for God has the power to subdue and subsume all worldly desires and, when it becomes intense enough, it leads to God-realization, bringing a permanent end to all sorrow and recovering our innate freedom, joy and fulfillment. This is the process that largely occurs in bhakti yoga.

Another way is to turn inward in deep contemplation, study the contents of one's mind and see how a desire, originating from one or more mental impressions, rises from the unconscious to the conscious mind and, when chosen by the will, becomes an intention which then leads to action. The effort here is to acquire control over one's will and make conscious effort not to engage it with destructive desires that arise in the mind. When not engaged, there is no intention (hence no action) and the desire sinks back into the unconscious. Later practices then deal with the elimination of mental impressions. This is the approach followed in rāja yoga.

In jñāna yoga the focus is not so much on *what* is desired as on *who* is desiring it. Using the incisive power of the purified intellect, one discovers that the "real me" is covered by layers of the ego, mind, body etc. Working in tandem, these produce a false identity which is very different from one's true identity, indeed even diametrically opposed to it. It is in this false identity that desires arise and sorrow is experienced. So the effort here is to let go of the false identity and regain one's true identity. Detaching oneself from the desirer automatically accomplishes detachment from desires.

While belief in a personal aspect of God is not prohibited in karma yoga, it is not mandatory. A karma yogi who does not believe in a personal God is expected to use his or her willpower to say a determined no to desires. But why would this person want to say no to desires? Stubbornly practical, karma yoga wants us to learn from our experiences in life. If there is one thing that is obvious—and yet almost always ignored—it is that a mind filled with desires is a mind that lacks peace and contentment. As desires increase, so do anxiety, stress and pain.[1] In karma yoga the effort is to detach oneself from desires every time they arise in one's mind. It is a continual practice, done with patience and perseverance. It calls for constant vigilance, making every moment a kind of inner awakening.[2]

Karma and Desire

Desire is usually demonized in religious literature. So let's think about it some more: What produces desires and where do they originate? All actions, physical and mental, lead to two kinds of results: one, the fruit of action (*karma-phala*) and, two, the mental impression (*saṁskāra*). The fruit of action is essentially an experience of joy or sorrow which comes sooner or later. The mental impression is the seed that lodges itself in the deeper layers of the mind.[3] It is from this mental impression that, given the right kind of stimulus, desire sprouts. The stimulus can be an external object grasped by the senses or a past memory awakened in the mind.

For example, when I eat ice cream and like it, the action produces both joy ("fruit of action") and a seed ("mental impression"). The next time I see ice cream somewhere, it provides the right stimulus for the seed in my mind to sprout as a desire to eat more ice cream. The seed of a pleasant experience produces the desire to *replicate* the experience by repeating the action. The seed of an unpleasant experience, on the other hand, produces the desire to *avoid* the experience by doing whatever it takes to avoid it. Regardless of the nature of the experience which produced the seed, every desire potentially leads to some kind of action.

Like a bubble that rises to the top of boiling water, the desire comes to the conscious part of my mind and then I become aware of it. I can choose to either ignore it or act upon it. If I decide to act upon it, my desire matures into intention, which leads to action, tightening the grip of the karma chain upon me. For, then I go eat more ice cream, get more joy, and add one more seed to the existing stock in my mind, which later will sprout as desire again. If I had only one ice cream seed in my mind before, I now have two, hence the chance of the desire sprouting is doubled. On and on and on, this process continues and I keep piling more and more seeds. What will happen to me is obvious: unless I try to arrest this process, I will get pushed around by my desires throughout my life, knowing precious little of what real contentment means. This is not a big problem if we are only dealing with ice cream! But we know that our desires go way beyond ice cream and can hurtle us into a potentially self-injurious abyss.

It is important to keep in mind the distinct functions of karma and the mental impression it produces. My past karma *determines* my present experience of joy and sorrow: the experience cannot be changed.[4] My mental impression, on the other hand, *influences*—it does not determine—my action through the kind of desire it generates. As we have seen, the desire for ice cream may propel me toward eating it, but it cannot force me to do so. I have the freedom to say a firm "no" to my desire. Using my willpower I can refuse to surrender to the desire and there the matter ends. The desire disappears but is not destroyed. It is reabsorbed into the mental impression and, given a suitable stimulus, may sprout again in future. The exercise of will, therefore, is very important in karma yoga, since it is the will that chooses which desire should lead to action and which desire should be squashed.

Moreover, we have the freedom to control the composition of our mental impressions, since they result from our own thoughts and actions. The totality of these mental impressions at any given time determines a person's character. If the majority of these impressions are good, positive and healthy, the person is said to have a good character. If the majority of the mental impressions are bad, negative and unhealthy, we say that the person has a bad character.[5]

The more our thoughts and actions are positive, healthy and good, the more our mental impressions will be positive, healthy and good. The less we think and act negatively and in an unhealthy manner, the less negative and unhealthy mental impressions we produce. In this way we can alter the composition of the impressions in our minds. None of us can claim to have our character carved in stone. Not for nothing is it said that every saint had a past and every sinner has a future.[6]

Desires are a "problem" not only because they snatch away our peace of mind but also because they are potential seeds of future sorrow when channeled through karma and rebirth. Not all desires are problematic though. What if a certain desire will not be the seed of future sorrow? The desire for God, for instance. Or the desire to be spiritually free. Obviously, these kinds of desires are not a problem at all. On the contrary, an intense desire to be free (*mumukṣutva*) or an intense desire for God (Sri Ramakrishna called it *vyākulatā*) is one of the primary requirements to reach the goal of yoga. Although these are "desires," they are by no means problematic.[7] There is no reason why a karma yogi would want to say "no" to these desires. In fact, these desires need an enthusiastic and emphatic "yes."

Then there are other desires—normally considered good —which are both helpful and problematic, thankfully not at the same time. These good desires are helpful in the beginning and can become problematic later. The desire to serve one's family, the desire to help the needy, the desire to be honest and truthful, the desire to go to heaven— these are clearly good desires and, when they lead to appropriate activity, they achieve a lot of individual and collective good. Such good actions propelled by good desires come under the purview of *dharma,* a blanket term in Sanskrit which stands for everything that is right and good in matters of justice, duty, responsibility, and work. Its exact opposite is *adharma,* meaning everything that is wrong and bad, everything which promotes injustice, dereliction of duty, shirking of responsibility, and destructive activity.

Desires that promote *dharma* are good and desires that promote *adharma* are bad. Good desires lead to good karma and result in temporal joy in this world or the next ("heaven"). Bad desires lead to bad karma and result in temporal sorrow in this world or the next ("hell"). Both kinds of desires keep the person tied to the "circle of relative existence," for even heavens and hells belong to the circle,[8] and every point on the circle is suffused with existential sorrow.

How can a "heaven" be a place of sorrow?[9] We know from our experience in the world that inequality is a major source of sorrow. It is inequality that breeds envy, jealousy and hatred—which often evolves into fights, quarrels, even wars. In descriptions and myths associated with heavens we see a hierarchy: happiness and pleasure are granted in proportion to the amount of good a person has done. Just as punishments in hell are given depending on how evil the person was, rewards in heaven are granted depending on how good the person was. This generates inequality even in heaven and, if our present experience is any guide, it is not unreasonable to expect envy and jealousy, and the consequent sorrow, even in heaven. This concern is reflected in many stories and myths related to heaven.

Moreover, the stay in heaven is limited, since it is unreasonable to expect infinite joy from the finite amount of good we do in the world.[10] So when the day of departure from heaven draws near, sorrow is the natural result. Most importantly, even in a heaven, we need a body to enjoy all the pleasures. Getting inside a body—that is, "being born" —involves taking upon oneself all the limitations of the body. This, as we have already seen, means dealing with illness, aging and death, not to speak of anxiety, stress and fear. This holds true whether one is born here or in some heaven.

This is the problematic part of even good desires. A gold chain is as much a chain as an iron one. No matter with what chain a person is tied, the result is the same: loss of freedom.[11] It sounds odd, but in spiritual life a point is reached when "good" ceases to be good and becomes a burden instead. The pairs of opposites, such as "good" and "bad," become meaningless in the nondual realm.

While *cultivating good desires* is essential for moral life, *eliminating all desires* is essential for spiritual life. Obviously, eliminating *all* desires is a tall order and seems not only unreasonable but also impossible. No one is expected to do it right away. Nor is it possible to do so. Since the edifice of spiritual life is built on a strong moral foundation, it is natural and customary for those on the spiritual path to cultivate good desires in the beginning, recognizing that eventually even these good desires will have to be transcended in order to realize the Ātman, our true self. For the Ātman is beyond good and bad, beyond all polarities, beyond both *dharma* and *adharma*.[12] All good desires, when pursued without any selfish motive, lead to purification of the heart, which is the prime prerequisite for spiritual development.[13]

If all desires have to be ultimately transcended, why bother to first cultivate good desires and eliminate bad ones? It would seem practical to skip the interim step and save both time and energy. Why not just go ahead and transcend whatever desires we have, good or bad? While this sounds logical enough, that's not how it works in practice. The trouble is that it is possible to transcend good desires but not bad ones. The bad ones have be rooted out through discernment and cultivation of good desires. The more time and energy we employ in pursuing good desires, the less time and energy we will have left at the service of bad desires. The power of *dharma* can transcend good desires and actions; *adharma* doesn't have that power. It's a little bit like the difference between rewards and punishments. If you are punished for a crime that you committed, you cannot refuse the punishment, but if you are rewarded for some achievement, you have the privilege to refuse the reward.

Karma and Love

A related question is, with all this talk about transcending desire, what happens to love? Since karma yoga recommends detachment, how can it have any place for love? Not to worry, there is plenty of love in the practice of karma yoga. Detachment and love can and do coexist. In fact, outrageous though it may sound, love can flourish only when there is true detachment. What cannot coexist with detachment is attachment, and much of what goes by the name "love" is really nothing but attachment. True love is rare, and blessed is the person who can truly love.[14]

Seeing an ad that said, "Your money will love our bank," a friend wrote me recently that "love" is a horribly abused word. It is difficult to argue with that. Viewed superficially, love and attachment look alarmingly similar. When we look deeply, however, their differences become obvious. The first thing we notice is that a person in the grip of attachment is primarily attached to "I", his or her pampered self, whereas one who is truly in love seldom thinks of the "I"—it's all about "you," the object of love.[15] The second thing we notice is that the attachment to "I" produces tentacles of ownership: one who is attached wants to own people and things, and make them "mine."[16] One who truly loves doesn't own anybody: a person in love respects freedom, one's own and others', so no one is tied with the noose of ownership.[17]

The difference between attachment and love becomes even more apparent in the results they produce. Attachment can —and often does—lead to dependence, anxiety, anger, jealousy and stress. Love, on the other hand, leads to deeper happiness and greater freedom.[18] Most relationships in life give rise to both joy and anxiety, a sense of freedom and, curiously, also a sense of bondage, occasional fulfillment and also bouts of anger. Which simply means that most relationships are a mixture of both love and attachment, each producing its results. Attachment stifles love and, if left unchecked, can destroy it. The problems in relationships are caused by attachment, not by love. The more the love in a relationship, the greater is the experience of happiness and freedom.

Since happiness and freedom are what result from the practice of karma yoga as well, it is easy to see why it deplores attachment and recommends detachment from desire. How important love is in karma yoga is best seen in the practice of detachment from karma.

Detachment from Karma

We have seen how the four yogas provide different ways to accomplish detachment from desire. The uniqueness of karma yoga lies, not surprisingly, in its special focus on developing techniques for detachment from karma. There are at least two major ways of detaching ourselves from karma: one way is for those who do not believe in a personal God, and the other is for those who do.

Here I must explain my use of the terms "believer" and "God." Let me begin with "believer" when used in connection with God. The word "believer" has undergone so much dilution over the years that today it means very little, if it means anything at all beyond affirming one's religiosity. Just as the term "non-believer" means little more than affirming one's rejection of religion and, paradoxically, making the person a believer in the nonexistence of God.

In Vedanta the word "belief" is used with great caution: it is not meant to be taken lightly. It is not something that can be switched on or off at will. Belief in God implies the deepest conviction that God exists. It is not a matter of hope. It is not also a pious wish or a periodic acknowledgment made when we pray or stand before the altar. The conviction that God exists is not intellectual either, although deep thinking may have helped the process. It is certainly not the result of a mystical experience of God, not yet anyway. This kind of conviction is ingrained in a person's mental makeup to such an extent that God becomes at least as real as the world. In time, this deep conviction or faith may evolve into seeing God as more real than the world. The Sanskrit word for this kind of conviction is *śraddhā*, which is explained as "the conviction in the existence" of God.[19] It is *śraddhā* that is the starting point of religious life in the truest sense of the term.

"God" is a tricky word, since it is understood in diverse ways by different people. In this book I use the term "God" to refer to the transcendent reality, which is *more real* than the world we encounter around us. The problem with the phrase "transcendent reality" is that it conjures up an abstract, ambiguous something which is not living and conscious. Nor would a phrase identifying God as a person solve the problem because, while it would obviously make God living and conscious, it would also circumscribes God's infinitude by ascribing qualities and gender to God.

This is a problem related to language, not to the truth the phrase is trying to express. The transcendent reality, or "God," in Vedanta is the Life of life.[20] God is not just conscious but is consciousness itself. God is the consciousness in all conscious beings.[21] Since we humans are not only living beings but also conscious beings, to us it has always seemed more easy and natural to visualize the transcendent reality as a living, conscious person.

When perceived as a "person," meaning someone with qualities (*saguna*) and/or with form (*sākāra*), the transcendent reality is known as the personal God (*īśvara* or *saguna brahman*). When viewed as a being without qualities (*nirguna*) and without form (*nirākāra*), the transcendent reality is known as the impersonal God, or the Absolute (*nirguna brahman*).

As perceptions, both the personal and the impersonal views are valid and authentic—and that's about the best the human mind can do in its attempts to understand God. To leap beyond the personal and the impersonal readings of God is to cross the limits of logic and enter the realm of direct experience (*anubhūti*). What is experienced in the state of transcendence is known only to the person who experiences it. No words can capture the experience fully. Language is too frail a vehicle to carry the load of that transcendent experience. Besides, how can anyone, or any language, express what is essentially inexpressible? No wonder that "the letter killeth."[22]

While *śraddhā* is essential in the practice of karma yoga, belief in a personal God is not. Detachment from karma for those who don't believe in a personal God occurs through a method called "work for work's sake."[23] For those who do believe in a personal God, the method is to do "work as an offering to God."

1. "Work for Work's Sake"

There is an ancient saying in Sanskrit, "Even a fool does not do anything without a motive." We all have motives behind everything we do. Much of our daily work and a considerable amount of our time are devoted to earning our livelihood, and the motive for this is obvious: to pay our bills, maintain our families, and survive in the marketplace of the world. Besides earning money, we also do a host of other things, and none of those things is motiveless.[24] Motives power the work and bind the person who does that work.

Motives are inevitably related to goals. When there are goals, they are either reached or not reached, resulting in what we call either success or failure, which in turn produces either joy or sorrow—all of this keeps us tied to the mesmerizing circle of karma and its effects.

Is it possible to *not* get enmeshed in the web of motive > work > results? The answer is yes. We can retain our freedom by doing work for work's sake. In other words, karma yoga recommends that the only "motive" (if we must use the word) powering our work should be the simple conviction that it is good to do what is good.[25] Or, what amounts to the same, the conviction that it is right to do what is right. No other reason, no other motive should color our activities.[26] We should simply choose to remain on the *dharma* path, because that is the only path worth walking on. We should not even expect gratitude.[27] On the contrary, it is we who should be grateful for every opportunity we get to practice *dharma.*[28] When we do work for work's sake and not for any selfish motive, it produces purity of mind (*cittaśuddhi*), a vital prerequisite for spiritual freedom.

Each of us may have our own idea about what is "good" and what is "right." How can I be sure that what I view as good and right is *really* good and right? As we have seen, the Sanskrit term *dharma* stands for everything that is good and right. A karma yogi follows the path of *dharma.* It is through scripture (*śāstra*), reason (*yukti*), and experience (*anubhūti*) that we learn what *dharma* is. Our learning of the *dharma* path may begin with books and generally with the guidance we receive from trusted mentors in our formative years, but reason takes over as soon as we are able to think clearly. It doesn't take a karma yogi too long to realize that what is good and right includes *everything* in life that makes us more unselfish and *nothing* that makes us injure others in thought, word or deed.[29] Although these are broad generalizations, they serve well as working guidelines. Eventually our own life experience will teach us, if nothing else does, what is truly good and right and what only appears to be so.

As karma yogis we are expected to do what is good and right, and then step aside without seeking any reward, any recognition, any gratitude. Our not seeking reward, recognition and gratitude doesn't mean they won't come. They well may and generally do. But if they don't, as karma yogis we won't care. The joy of consciously doing what is good and what is right is itself so abundant and powerful that it prevents us from being perturbed by indifference, neglect, even criticism. Believing in the wisdom of the scriptures helps. We remember the promise found in the *Gītā* (6.40): "The doer of good never comes to grief," and the assurance of the Vedas: "Truth alone triumphs, not untruth."[30]

This is obviously not easy to practice. A person who wants to work for work's sake must have enormous conviction in the power of goodness,[31] stoic forbearance toward the vagaries of the world,[32] and self-confidence which is strong enough to remain unaffected by praise or blame.[33] Such a person loves what is good and what is right for its own sake, recognizing that the life based on truth and goodness is its own reward. Such a life purifies the heart: it frees the mind of its burdens, making us lighter and the world brighter. When we work for work's sake, we are able to minimize and finally crush the spiritually paralyzing mischief of our headstrong ego, and this effectively produces detachment from karma.

2. "Work as an Offering to God"

The second way of detaching from karma is for those who believe in a personal God. This method consists of doing all work as an offering to God.[34] All work is God's work.[35] Doing work is an honor, a privilege, an opportunity. God exists in everyone and in everything. We cannot help anyone, we can only serve. Since we are really dealing with God alone, no matter where we work or what work we do, all service is really a form of worship.[36] Doing work as worship is an effortless way to detach oneself from karma.

How does this detachment occur? In the early stages, doing things for oneself or for others ("work") and doing things for God or out of love for God ("worship") remain separate initiatives, each requiring its own quota of time and energy. People often confront dilemmas or experience stress while trying to figure out how to balance the two, work and worship. We enter the second stage when we make a conscious effort to do work *as* worship. If I owe everything to God including my own existence, then even I don't belong to myself. In that case, is my work really "my" work? If all are God's children, isn't working for others the same as working for God's children? If God dwells in me and in everyone and everything in the world, then no matter who I am dealing with and who I am working for, I am really dealing only with God and working only for God. In which case, what I see as "work" becomes nothing more and nothing less than "worship." This is the third stage, the realization that work *is* worship.

Understanding this theoretically does not of course mean that it is easy to practice it. Habits die hard. Only a conscious and determined effort by a person filled with *śraddhā* makes it possible to begin doing work *as* worship. Every work, no matter how insignificant, should be done as an offering to God. Usually this means doing work as an offering to one's *iṣṭa*, one's chosen ideal through which God is manifested. Seeing God in every person and in every object is the key to this practice.

A physician karma yogi's worship will have medical examination and medicines as an offering to God who appears as a sick person. A teacher karma yogi will worship the student-God through the offering of education. If there is any work that cannot be done as an offering to God, or out of love for God, a karma yogi shouldn't be doing it. Sri

Ramakrishna called this "work as worship" practice *śiva-jñāne jīvasevā,* "serving all beings with the knowledge that they are manifestations of God."

Much effort is needed in the beginning, as it is easy to forget and lapse into old habit-driven methods of work. But gradually, with purity of purpose and indomitable grit, with patience and perseverance, it becomes progressively easier to do all work as worship. When this becomes effortless and natural, we realize in the depths of our being that work *is* worship when it is done out of love for God and as an offering to God. When the love is missing, even worship becomes a chore, a "work" that needs to be done. When the heart is filled with love for God, every work becomes an act of worship. What the ignorant call "work" is nothing but "worship" in the eyes of the enlightened.

We have seen that to break the karma chain, we must attack its weakest link, the link that connects desire with karma. This is accomplished through a twofold practice of detachment: detachment from desire and detachment from karma. All four yogas have their specialized approaches to developing detachment from desire. But detachment from karma is where karma yoga lays special emphasis and the two principal methods employed are "work for work's sake" and doing "work as an offering to God."

Both these methods spring from love. Doing work for work's sake becomes possible only for the person who truly loves what is right and good for its own sake. Doing work as worship, or as an offering to God, becomes possible only for the person who truly loves God and sees the divine presence in everyone and everything. These two methods accomplish more than merely detachment from karma. They also simultaneously eliminate the attachment to the doer of karma ("I") and to the results of karma.

While the basic theoretical framework of the karma yoga practice has been laid out in the preceding pages, we need to turn our attention now to the practice itself. An ounce of practice is worth tons of theory.[37] As a spiritual practice, yoga frees us from the shackles of ignorance and restores our true nature, which is being (*sat*), consciousness (*cit*), bliss (*ānanda*) absolute. Two things are especially important in this quest for freedom: detachment (*vairāgya*) and practice (*abhyāsa*).[38] We have seen what detachment can do. Now we need to turn to practice.

A major challenge in spiritual life is not the understanding of principles but their implementation in practice. How can we transform abstract principles into practicable and effective techniques? This is something that all spiritual seekers have to do themselves. Books can provide insights but the readers needs to *apply* the insights to their own specific life situations and evolve methods that will work for them. The following chapter, in some ways the heart of this manual, will address the question of the reader who says, "The insights of karma yoga appeal to my mind and heart. I want to practice karma yoga. How should I begin and what should I do?"

FOUR

Practice

---

*U*sually the first question related to a Vedanta spiritual practice is about eligibility. Who is eligible to practice karma yoga? What are the basic requirements to be a fit candidate (*adhikāri*) for the practice? The first obvious requirement is interest: the karma yoga principles must resonate with our own vision of spiritual life. You and I already have interest in karma yoga. Without it, I wouldn't have cared to write this book and you wouldn't have cared to pick it up.

The second requirement is a resolute determination to reach the goal. How strong is my urge to be spiritually free and how strong my determination to do whatever it takes to attain freedom? This is the question each of us has to ask ourselves. The answer to this question is important, since the success in our practice and the speed with which it is attained depend on it.

The third requirement is faith in oneself and faith in God. If we don't have faith in ourselves, then our faith in God is not of much value.[1] As we have seen, faith in a personal

God is not mandatory for the practice of karma yoga, but faith, or *śraddhā*, in a higher reality is a must. Which is not to say that without it one cannot work selflessly. What it does mean is that without *śraddhā* our selfless work won't be karma yoga.

Interest, determination, and *śraddhā*—these, then, are what make a person eligible for karma yoga practice. According to Vedanta texts, every activity occurs through three channels: body (*kāyā*), mind (*manas*) and speech (*vāk*). It is through these three channels that we communicate with others and through which all of our interactions with the world take place. Sri Ramakrishna often advised his students to "make the mind and speech one," in other words, to make sure that there is harmony between our thoughts and our words.[2]

What creates stress and produces tension is the lack of harmony between what we *think* and what we *say* and what we *do*. Our thoughts, words and actions go in different directions. The result is a life that lacks focus and authenticity. The most important requirement for a budding karma yogi is to strive to make the mind, body and speech conform to one another.

Detachment, the key to karma yoga, must manifest strongly and equally through our thoughts, words and actions. It must express itself through how we think and what we say. It must shine through everything that we do. At present our thoughts, words and actions showcase how attached we are. If we are not mindful, we may not even be aware of the enormous burden of attachments each of us is relentlessly carrying every moment, day after day, from birth to death and to birth again. These attachments spring from an unreflective, stubborn "I" and the tentacles of ownership that it spreads on everything it perceives as "mine." "I and mine" rule our lives and snuff out its pure joys and freedoms. The practice of karma yoga is a practice that throws off this dead-weight burden of attachments. The only way to remove attachments is through a conscious practice of detachment.[3]

Detachment through the Mind

How do we detach from the "I" mentally? The process is simple enough in telling but practicing it needs enormous patience and perseverance. Just as a wrongly addressed letter or email is rejected and bounced back to the sender, all praise and blame addressed to the "I" are to be rejected and bounced back to their source. After all, whatever work is accomplished in karma yoga is done out of love for *dharma* ("work for work's sake") or out of love for God ("work as an offering to God"), and the singular focus of one in love is not "I" but "you"—and the "you" here is either God or *dharma*. The more the "I" goes out, the more does God or *dharma* come in.

It is the nature of the world to shower praise or heap blame, and every person has plenty of both in the course of a lifetime. Oddly enough, the same work may at times elicit praise from some and blame from others. Most people have no problem with praise: the more the praise, the merrier they feel. It is blame that is problematic: it puts people on the defensive. But if I am greedy for praise, then I will be fearful of criticism and, when criticism comes, I'll be miserable. To spare myself the fear, the anxiety and the consequent misery, I must find a way to deal intelligently with both praise and blame. Karma yoga's prescription is simple and direct: make an effort to remain unaffected by both. That is what bouncing back both praise and blame means.[4]

Introspection helps in dealing with praise and blame. What is behind all the praise? If it is only a courtesy gesture, not quite uncommon in today's corporate and increasingly shallow culture, it is not meant to be taken seriously. The praiser forgets it in no time and the praised should do likewise. If the praise is genuine, it reflects appreciation for *dharma,* meaning that which is good and right. To the extent it inspires the praiser to emulate the example, the praiser is benefited and the world becomes ever so slightly a better place to live in. There is no reason whatsoever, though, for the karma yogi to be puffed up by praise. If that happens, the "I" rises to the surface and the "yoga" part of the work disappears, leading eventually to sorrow, the opposite of the longed-for outcome.

What is behind all the blame? Either the blame is deserved or not deserved. If the blame is deserved, the karma yogi acknowledges the mistake and does everything to rectify the error to the extent possible. The karma yogi also resolves to be more alert and not make the same mistake again. If the blame is not deserved, the karma yogi smiles and moves on, without being defensive and without protest. Life is too short to be spent in trying to convince others about how blameless we are.

In this way both praise and blame are bounced off and the mind learns to detach itself from "I and mine." Attachments can arise in other ways as well: this is *my* work, these are *my* people, this is *my* family. The mind practicing detachment deals with these thoughts through constant self-reminders such as: this is *God's* work, I am only an instrument. These people are *God's* children and I am here to serve. This is not my family, but *God's* gift which I am privileged to take care of.[5] Those who don't believe in a personal God strengthen their "attachment" to *dharma* to such an extent that all other attachments become irrelevant and inconsequential.

The idea of duty is another attachment-inducing bug in the mind.[6] Different duties come to us at different stages in life and we must carry them out to the best of our ability. But how helpful is it to see our work as our "duty"? Not much, really. If we love the work, we do it anyway, duty or not. If we don't love the work, we do it reluctantly, as something that we'd rather avoid but can't. Such forced labor brings no joy.[7] The karma yogi tries to do work out of love, not out of compulsion. Only the work that is done out of love is liberating.[8] We must work like a master, not as a slave.[9]

If we must do something, why not find ways to *want* to do it instead of dragging our feet unwillingly and doing it with grudging reluctance? If we don't get to do what we love, ways must be found to love what we've to do, first, because there may be no other option, and more importantly second, because in karma yoga it is not so much *what* we do that matters as *how* we do it.[10] We hardly need a reminder at this point that if the action is not ethical and appropriate, it won't qualify as karma yoga no matter *how* it is done.

Doing work out of a sense of duty is not wrong, of course. Done sincerely and with a spiritual goal in view, it can purify the mind and evolve into work without any sense of duty.[11] Even when engaged in carrying out duties, a karma yogi makes a conscious effort to rise above the idea of duty and to do everything out of love—love for God or love for *dharma*.

From the spiritual standpoint, doing work as "duty" is a slave's work and that is what most people do everywhere. Duties take over our lives. They leave us no time to do what we really want to do. Some duty or other drags us every moment, at every step, in every place. A lifetime filled with duties—the horror of it![12] Why not find ways to work out of love and freedom? Developing the right attitude toward work is therefore an important practice in karma yoga.[13]

Another helpful practice is to remember that everything passes away, nothing lasts forever. The less we forget this, the more detached we become. Being detached is not the same as being indifferent. The two are not intrinsically connected. It is possible to be intensely interested in something and also deeply aware that it won't last forever. In fact, it is this deep awareness of fragility and mortality embedded in the fabric of the world that helps us appreciate the value of everyone and everything that we see as "our" or "mine"—and this includes our possessions, our friends, our family. Because these won't be around forever, we deal with them with understanding, compassion, love— and spare ourselves the regret and repentance that can occur for not doing the right thing when it was possible. Not to forget what each of us sees as "my" body will pass away too. Detachment must be as vigorously applied to oneself as we apply it to others. Awareness of impermanence helps in maintaining detachment.

Detachment through Speech

Detachment through speech flows naturally from mental detachment. When our mind and speech are in harmony, our speech becomes an expression of our thoughts. Our detached attitude to life is effortlessly reflected in the way we use our words and the way we utter them. What if our mind and speech are yet to become harmonious? This is very likely the case in the initial stages of our practice, when the mind is making an effort—not always successfully —to practice detachment. The efforts of the mind can be supplemented and supported by consciously employing speech to reflect one's detachment.

This does not, of course, mean that we should eliminate from our vocabulary words such as "me" or "mine," words that indicate possession, words that virtually breathe attachment. It's not the *words* that communicate, it's the *person* behind the words who does. If words were all that mattered, sweet talkers would have ruled the roost. That seldom happens. It is the person uttering the words that determines how effective they are. At the Parliament of Religions in 1893, when Vivekananda began his talk with, "Sisters and brothers of America," the electrifying impact was not due to the words but due to the person who uttered them. Merely refusing to use the words "I," "me" and "mine" will not eliminate the idea of possession from our hearts. It is possible to use those words without being possessive and attached.

And yet no one can deny the power of words. Our lives are filled with words and symbols. Both words and symbols are crystallized thoughts. Not many people realize how much is being revealed about them through the words they use and the symbols they employ.[14] The sound of a word, its meaning, the images it evokes, and the word itself are interrelated. A well-written novel, a thoughtful lecture, a persuasive argument, or a moving confession can be amazingly powerful. Recognizing the immense power that words have, a karma yogi uses words with great care. A careless remark or a rash and vocal judgment or an over-the-top emotional outburst returns to haunt us sooner or later. Using words responsibly is an integral part of karma yoga practice.[15]

Silence can often be more eloquent than words. It also affords the karma yogi the necessary space and time to reflect before responding to the events outside. The practice of silence (*mauna*) is helpful in preserving one's detached frame of mind and protecting oneself from being carried away by the force of instinctive reflexes and knee-jerk reactions. It is helpful to practice silence periodically, observing a day of silence once a fortnight or once a month. If that seems impracticable, then even a few minutes of silence everyday or an hour of silence once a week can be immensely helpful.

Such a practice would include not only not speaking but also switching off one's phone, computer, radio and TV. If I get bored during this practice, it simply means that my own company is awfully boring. On the other hand, if I relish the inner and outer silence, it means that my company is enjoyable. If I enjoy my own company, chances are that others will enjoy it too when I emerge from my period of silence. As Swami Vivekananda pointed out, "Out of purity and silence comes the word of power."[16]

A simple rule of thumb about speaking is this: if my words are likely to heal, help or ease a given situation, I must speak. If not, I must hold my silence. If this rule is taken to heart, we may find ourselves listening more and talking less, which in itself is a wonderful practice, promoting both peace and calm detachment. There is a saying in Bengali, "A mute person has no enemies."

Besides, a good listener generally accomplishes more than a rabid talker. The practice of "listening" is thus an integral part of karma yoga. A karma yogi listens, reflects, talks only when needed and, most importantly, *does* what is right and appropriate. One may go to the extent of saying that a karma yogi "talks" more through detached action than through superfluous words.[17]

In the customary reference to the threefold activities of body, mind and speech, "speech" represents all the senses (*indriya*), not just itself. The senses are generally said to be ten, divided into two groups: five senses of knowledge (*jñānendriya*) and five senses of action (*karmendriya*).[18] The senses have specialized functions and they are tied to the body and mind in carrying out their functions. What makes "speech" stand out among all the senses is that it plays the most radical role in articulating thoughts or hiding them and in building relationships or snapping them. That is why it is helpful to take a special look at speech when we are dealing with the senses.

Detachment through Action

Like speech, our actions are also expressions of our thoughts. The thoughts, words and actions of a person together constitute who that person is at any given moment. The actions of one who is detached will invariably be detached, leaving no residue of any kind.

Actions often produce inner reactions such as anxiety, exhilaration or regret: anxiety if there is no certainty about the result; exhilaration when successful or in anticipation of a reward; and regret upon failure or when life looks anything but rosy. A truly detached action is completely free from anxiety, exhilaration and regret. The practice therefore involves doing every work as best we can but not with any ulterior motive other than doing good because it is good to do good ("work for work's sake") or doing work out of love for God ("work as an offering to God").

The ideal is to work hard but not seek the results of work.[19] It is the attachment to results that binds us. It fills us with anxiety and produces physical and mental stress. It prevents us from giving ourselves fully to the work in hand. We must be detached from the *results* of work but not from the work itself.[20] Since no one can remain without work even for a moment, it is better to engage oneself in work which is both ethical and useful. Questioning the rationale behind every work is an important karma yoga practice.

Work everybody does, but only the work that is done as a science, work that is efficient in every way, transforms it from ordinary karma to karma *yoga*.[21] The "science" behind work is simple: if my work produces fulfillment instead of anxiety and aggravated stress levels, then it is truly detached work. It means my work is being done as yoga. Thus, what inner experience my work habits produce provides a good litmus test to determine whether my actions are truly detached.

Karma yoga does not mean merely working hard. Workaholics are not necessarily karma yogis. Working compulsively is a kind of disease (*roga*), not a spiritual practice (*yoga*).

Karma Yoga Practice

The practice of karma yoga is the practice of detachment, which is the only way to break the chain that binds us to the karma cycle. We have seen some of the basic elements involved in the practice of detachment through the mind, speech and action. These basic elements need to become tangible, they need to be fleshed out, and they need to be customized to our specific needs.

Every one of us is unique. Not only do we look different but our life situations are also different, as are our specific ways of understanding the world, our style of dealing with it, and our needs, fears and hopes. Spiritual seekers have to find ways to transform abstract philosophical principles and insights into workable practices suited to their own life situations. This is something each of us has to do on our own. No teacher will do it for us. No book can do it for us.

Nevertheless, it is still possible to produce a template which is flexible enough for individual customization. Here is an attempt to produce one possible template for karma yoga practice.

As we have seen, an important requirement for a successful karma yoga practice is to harmonize the functions of the mind, speech and body. Our practice therefore should integrate our thoughts, words and actions into a wholesome way of living and doing. Karma yoga practice, like any good spiritual discipline, is not divorced from one's "normal" life but is the engine that drives and nourishes it.

DAILY PRACTICE
Morning

The practice ideally begins with self-reminders. A karma yogi makes the following affirmations before beginning the activities for the day. One who believes in God can make these affirmations after the morning prayers, repetition of mantra (*japa*) and meditation. Others can simply find a quiet spot for the practice. In either case, a lighted incense helps create the right environment. At the end of every affirmation, the karma yogi offers a flower before one's personal shrine, or bows down to the infinite presence of *dharma*.

With a calm and focused mind, the karma yogi makes the following resolves.

1. "I resolve to be mindful of the *motive* behind my work. I will examine my motives to make sure that they are in harmony with my spiritual ideal.
2. "I resolve to be mindful of the *nature* of my work. I will do only what is ethical and productive, and what does not violate my values and principles.
3. "I resolve to be mindful of the *quality* of my work. I will work with love and care, remembering that my happiness depends on it.
4. "I resolve to be mindful of the *approach* to my work. I will do my work as an offering to God (*or*, I will work for work's sake), expecting no rewards, seeking no favors, and avoiding no challenges.
5. "I resolve to be mindful of my *mind*. I will try to remain focused on the activity in hand and not allow the mind to be distracted.
6. "I resolve to be mindful of my *speech*. I will use my

words to heal and not hurt. I will try to listen carefully and act responsibly.

7. "I resolve to be mindful of my *actions*. I will be efficient and try to make the best use of my time and energy.

Throughout the Day

The karma yogi makes a determined effort to remain alert, calm and cheerful throughout the day. It is helpful to divide the day into segments, where each segment represents a distinct activity or a specific project. Even an arbitrary division of a day into 1- or 2- or 3- hour segments will do.

Before the beginning of each segment, the karma yogi quickly goes through the resolves made in the morning. There is no need to repeat them ritually as was done earlier in the day. Simply remembering the keyword in each resolve is enough of a self-reminder: motive, nature, quality, approach, mind, speech, and action. This might seem cumbersome and impractical, but with a little practice it becomes easy, feels natural and doesn't need more than a few seconds.

The benefit of every such self-reminder is immediate: it gathers the scattered mind back on the present activity and energizes it with renewed alertness and focus. The ease with which this is accomplished feels almost like a miracle.

Evening

When the major part of the day's work is over, it is time for the second set of karma yoga exercises. Devotees can do it before their evening practice of *japa* and meditation, and others can do it before retiring to bed.

The practice essentially consists of going over the day's activities in a fast-forward mode and asking questions. It is helpful to rate ourselves on the scale of 1 to 10, where 10 meets the requirement for a perfect practice of karma yoga. Or we can grade ourselves using other methods.

Not only does this develop the capacity of critical self-assessment but, done rightly, it creates the space between the observer-me and the worker-me, effectively loosening the hold of the ego on my self-identity.

Sitting calmly in a quiet spot, as in the morning, the karma yogi asks these questions:

1. Did I do anything today which would *not* qualify as ethical?
2. Did I work with love and care, giving full attention to the task in hand?
3. Did I work for work's sake, with no expectation of any kind? *or,* did I do my work as an offering to God?
4. Did I talk too much? Was I able to use my words to heal and help?
5. Did I handle praise and criticism with equanimity?
6. Did I make the best use of my time and energy?

The purpose of this exercise is neither to find an excuse to pat ourselves on the back nor to find reasons to feel guilty and feel depressed. The purpose is simply to know where we stand. No need to feel discouraged by the dismal score for the day.

The negatives of the day show us where we were wrong or what we could have done in a better way. We know then where we need to pay extra attention the following day. The positives of the day encourage us, for they confirm that we are on the right track. This boosts our confidence and fills our heart with joy.

The mistakes we make are the mistakes most people make anyway. Mistakes are a blessing, for they teach us what went wrong and what we should *not* do. The more the mistakes we make, the more we learn. But making the same mistake again and again is a different story. It's not a blessing obviously, but it can be a humbling revelation that we are not original even in our mistakes. It is also a warning that we have not learnt the lesson. We will understand eventually, if we haven't already, that we suffer when we don't learn the lessons life is trying to teach us, and we keep suffering until the lesson is learnt.

The karma yogi goes to sleep with a firm resolve to learn from the day's lessons and to improve the karma yoga score for the next day. Patience, perseverance, and purity of purpose—these are the guiding mottos of the karma yogi. Come morning, the karma yogi is ready to begin the day afresh, affirming the resolves with renewed determination and a joyful heart.

Alongside the set of daily practices, the karma yogi observes occasional periods of silence: this can be done once a week or a fortnight, or even for a short time every day, if possible. All electronic gadgets are switched off. A short inspirational reading, perhaps from a scripture of one's choice, is helpful to set the period of silence rolling. A quiet walk is helpful and simply sitting mindfully in one's room also helps. Through these periods of silence we can take stock of our lives and get to know ourselves better. The inner silence gives us an opportunity to get back to the core of our being, which is the source of all peace, purity and perfection.

As should be obvious by this time, the practice of karma yoga is much more than simply the phrase "be good and do good" may imply. Karma yoga is an intensely conscious practice, which demands relentless attention to the motives that prompt us to work, to the nature and quality of the work that we do, and to the harmony between speech, mind and body. It is a practice that can, when perfected, bring us the greatest prize of all—freedom in the truest sense of the term.

FIVE

Freedom

*I*s freedom really the greatest prize of all? It depends on who you ask. Not everyone sees freedom as the greatest prize or, for that matter, even simply as a prize. A prize is, after all, something that is avidly sought. We only seek what we need, and we only need what we lack. When we miss something most intensely and need it real badly, then we prize it above everything else. When we feel an acute sense of bondage, we become really hungry for freedom. We long for freedom as intensely as a person whose head is on fire would rush frantically to find water.[1] Only then does freedom appear to us as the greatest prize of all.

There are people who feel an acute sense of bondage and there are people who don't. Most people who are incarcerated know what bondage means and understand the value of freedom. Those who live and labor under severe financial constraints understand the value of economic freedom. Those who live in totalitarian states with draconian laws long for civic and political freedoms. In a domestic

setting, teenagers want to break free when they feel suffo-
cated by house rules imposed by their concerned parents.
More examples can easily be added, since there are as
many kinds of freedoms as there are bondages.

Karma and Freedom

So what kind of freedom does karma yoga practice lead
to? The answer is hidden in plain sight. Karma yoga practice leads to freedom from the bondage of karma. We have
seen how the karma chain binds us into this seemingly
never-ending roller coaster of relative existence. We are
pushed helplessly from birth to death and to birth again,
and are injected with alternate doses of joy and sorrow,
which fill our lives with hope and despair, each following
the other.

The core of our being—pure consciousness, or the Ātman
—seems trapped. Karma yoga frees this apparently bound
spirit from the clutches of the material world symbolized
by karma. Since it frees the spirit, it is spiritual freedom
that karma yoga practice leads to. Karma done the wrong
way binds the spirit, and karma done the right way—
which is what karma yoga is—frees the spirit.

Freedom, as a worthy goal to reach or a prize to be won,
becomes real only when the experience of bondage
becomes real. If we don't *feel* we are bound, we won't *feel*
any urge to become free. It is as simple as that. Most
people experience a sense of freedom in their personal
lives but oftentimes also some constraints. Depending on
how severe those constraints are, people strive to be free
from them. Since the constraints are seen as hurdles to
happiness, people end up pursuing pleasure, because it
seems to give instant happiness. Far from bringing happi-

ness though, a mindless pursuit of pleasure makes their lives even more miserable.[2]

While most people are sensitive to the limitations experienced in their daily lives, only a few have the deeper kind of sensitivity needed to feel the bondage inherent in human experience. This kind of bondage is *existential*, because it is embedded in our very existence as human beings. It is experienced as our lack of freedom from the reality of aging, sickness and death. At the mental level, there are limits to how much we can know and feel, and we have no freedom to overcome those limits. Beneath the superficial pretensions associated with life lies the usually unexpressed and mostly subliminal fear of death. The joy of being seems forever in tension with the fear of nonbeing. We are trapped within the domains of time, space and causality. Only to those who are awakened to this depressing reality of human existence does spiritual freedom become an urgent, compelling goal.

The experience of existential bondage can impinge on our consciousness in a general way or it can take any number of specific forms. For instance, if I am puzzled by the mystery of existence and dying to know what's what, I will soon find myself against a stone wall beyond which my intellect simply cannot go. I will realize the limits to which reasoning and logic can take me and will become frustrated by my ignorance. When this happens, my goal in life will be to attain knowledge. In other words, I will be seeking freedom from ignorance. In the same way, if I feel my imperfection intensely, the goal of my life will be to become perfect. No matter how I choose to express that goal, I will really be seeking freedom from imperfection.

Not everyone's goal in life is expressed in the same words. Among those who are spiritually inclined, some may see the goal as knowledge, others may see it as perfection, purity, or eternal bliss. Those who are theistically oriented may see the goal as being in heaven in the presence of God, or under the eternal care and love of the Divine Mother. Is this any different from seeking freedom from the limitations and travails of life in this world? Even a worldly goal, such as being wealthy or famous or getting a good job or an ideal spouse, is really the seeking of freedom from a specific, desire-propelled need. No goal can be imposed from the outside. Every one has to figure out for themselves what their specific goal in life is. Whichever way the goal is expressed, it is always some form of freedom that is being sought, consciously or unconsciously.[3]

Religions of the world describe their goals in various ways. At first glance, it is not easy to see how *nirvāṇa*, salvation and *mokṣa* could have anything in common. Each of these goals is defined in terms of the unique theology and world-view of a distinct religion. These goals cannot be easily equated or compared with one another. Stripped of their theological trappings and examined in experiential terms though, it is not too difficult to see freedom emerge as the key ingredient in them all.[4] It is possible to acknowledge the diversity of goals and yet affirm their unity in the experience of freedom. In theistic language, the goal is often identified with God, who is seen as the embodiment of freedom, knowledge, perfection, purity and bliss. In non-theistic language, Vedanta identifies the goal as simply freedom (*mokṣa* or *mukti*).

The truth is that all that exists has its origin in freedom, it seems to dwell for a time in the realm of bondage, and it returns to being free again.[5] That is the basic premise of

Vedantic thinking and the key phrase in the above sentence is "seems to dwell," meaning, it doesn't *really* dwell in the realm of bondage. In other words, it's freedom, freedom, freedom all the way. Just because bondage is felt doesn't make it real, anymore than a dream is real simply because it is seen. All paths of yoga help in eliminating this seeming bondage and restoring the freedom which was never lost. Yoga breaks the dream of bondage and awakens us to the reality that we are free.[6]

Guideposts

The karma chain is what binds us. It is snapped by breaking the link between desire and karma. As we have seen, detachment is the instrument used in karma yoga to break the link. Once that is accomplished, the Ātman—which is who you and I really are—returns to its native glory and basks in the sunshine of freedom. No one knows when this sunshine will illumine our hearts and lives. Sometimes it seems too distant a goal to qualify even as a dream. Our efforts may seem too inadequate to win so precious a prize. We may also wonder if we just have to grit our teeth, continue the practice, and keep waiting endlessly, hoping against hope, that somehow someday the clouds will disperse and our hearts will be flooded with the light of knowledge and freedom.

How would we even know that we are on the right track? How can we be sure that our practice is not off the mark? The spiritual teacher is the right person to gauge the extent of our progress and to correct us when we do something stupid. But we may not have the privilege of having the spiritual teacher by our side to guide us all the time. We need ways to self-test our progress. We need to know whether any guideposts exist in our spiritual journey. Fortunately they do.

Within a few days of earnest practice, almost the first thing we notice is how difficult it is to change our habits: how often our work is mechanical, our reactions instinctual, our thoughts chaotic, our speech hollow, and our motives selfish.[7] We notice how easy it is to forget the principles of karma yoga and how difficult to keep our thoughts, words and actions in sync.

This can be a discouraging discovery, but it is in fact an encouraging sign: for a change, we are now aware of the problem and that dramatically improves the odds of solving it. Ignorance may be bliss but not for too long, for the problem begins to stink after a while. Knowledge can be discomforting but it also opens the door to exciting solutions to the problem. The first sign that we are on the right track is that we discover the problem, acknowledge its presence, and become determined to solve it.

When we continue to practice with determination, undeterred by initial failures, we soon get into a routine. The challenge then is to remain alert that our practice doesn't become mechanical. The increased alertness improves the quality of our work and we begin to taste tiny bits of success in the practice. This produces not only inner joy but also greater calm.

Another sign of progress is that we are able to handle both praise and blame in a more mature way: praise does not turn our heads and blame does not make us angry or defensive. Our relationships improve and we are able to recover faster from our physical and mental exhaustion. We become more unselfish, and this enhances inner strength and improves our health.[8]

A much greater change occurs in the way we look at life and our place in it. This change happens over a period of time and takes a while before we even notice it. Those who "work for work's sake" find themselves contented and at peace with themselves and with the world. Seldom is their inner balance disturbed.[9] Those who do "work as an offering to God" find their devotion deepening and their spirit of surrender removing much of the stress and anxiety from their lives. Life becomes progressively more meaningful and joyful to the karma yogi who is on the right track.

When this process reaches its culmination, the karma chain is broken and the link connecting desire with karma is snapped. Freed from the shackles of birth and death, the karma yogi's mere presence becomes a blessing. Every thought the karma yogi thinks, every word that the karma yogi utters, and every work that the karma yogi does fills the world with the power of goodness and well-being.

When death eventually arrives, the karma yogi greets it fearlessly and departs with a smile. There is no more coming back. The karma yogi is free—forever. Every generation has at least a handful of people who have managed to break the karma chain and become spiritually free in this way. Most among these remain unknown to the world at large, but their presence in our midst is a blessing nonetheless.[10]

Exemplars

Among the karma yogis whose life and legacy have become well-known is Buddha. Swami Vivekananda identified him as the greatest karma yogi ever born, since Buddha embodied in fullest measure all the qualities associated with the practice of karma yoga. The story of Siddhartha's first encounter outside the palace with the sick, the aged and the dead may have been apocryphal but its message is clear: Siddhartha was a prince endowed with clear perception and deep thinking. He was able to see what most others could not: the obvious and yet hidden truth that the sorrow associated with illness, aging and death was inseparable from human existence. Siddhartha yearned to find the way out. With tremendous determination, which is the hallmark of karma yoga practice, he set forth and was able to find the way beyond suffering. That is how Siddhartha the prince became transformed into Buddha "the awakened."

As long as we are being controlled by karma we are asleep. When we break the karma chain, we wake up. Every one of us, therefore, is a potential Buddha. Buddha is not a person, it is a state of being. That is what Buddha reminded his disciples before his death.[11] Buddha's detachment from both desire and karma was so complete that he did not do anything in life with a selfish motive. Not for nothing did Swami Vivekananda say that Buddha represented the highest ideal of karma yoga.[12]

It needs no great imagination to see the amazing parallels between the personalities of Buddha and Vivekananda. While Buddha's life continues to inspire us even today, Vivekananda's does in a strikingly personal way. He is, after all, much closer to us in time and it is therefore easier to relate to him and identify with his inspiring life and powerful message. Like all great teachers, Vivekananda's own life is the best commentary on his teachings. The reason his exposition of karma yoga is so powerful is that he lived what he taught. Should there be any question regarding karma yoga practice, we only need to study Vivekananda's life to find the right answer.

Every great prophet and saint is a karma yogi in one form or another, even though karma yoga may not be the dominant characteristic of all of them. The benefit in looking at some of these great exemplars of the karma yoga tradition is that their lives not only inspire us but also educate us about the principles and practice of karma yoga. The goal is not simply to adore these enlightened beings but to become enlightened ourselves.

Enlightenment through karma yoga comes through breaking the karma chain with the ax of detachment. When the connection between desire and karma is broken, there is no longer any desirer or worker, which is how the Ātman had begun to sees itself through ignorance. The triad of work, the worker and the object of work is demolished. No longer is there any division between desire, the desirer and the object of desire. All that remains is the one being who is neither tormented by desire nor goaded to work. This one being is eternally pure and perfect, blissful and free. *You* are that free being. *I* am that free being. We all are that one free being. The return to being who we really are is the return to being simple again. Spiritual life is all about returning to our native simplicity. When we are simple, we are happy and free.

How, why and when we became complex and complicated we may never know, but we know now how to go back to being our true selves. The return journey may seem long, but no matter how long the way, it always begins with the first step. Teachers may inspire us. Books may educate us. But they cannot take that first step on our behalf. We have to do it ourselves. No one else can do it for us. The earlier we start, the better for us.

We have waited long enough. The tipping point has been reached. Let us shake off our physical and mental lethargy and start walking the walk to freedom. There is no time to lose.

The best time to begin the practice is now.

This very moment.

Notes

Preface

1. For an inspiring account of Goodwin's life and contribution to Vedanta, see Pravrajika Vrajaprana, *"My Faithful Goodwin"* (Kolkata: Advaita Ashrama, 1994). After Goodwin's death, Vivekananda wrote in a letter to Goodwin's mother in June 1898: "The debt of gratitude I owe him can never be repaid, and those who think they have been helped by any thought of mine ought to know that almost every word of it was published through the untiring and most unselfish exertions of Mr. Goodwin. In him I have lost a friend true as steel, a disciple of never-failing devotion, a worker who knew not what tiring was, and the world is less rich by one of those few who are born, as it were, to live only for others." CW, 9. 106–107.

2. Swami Vivekananda did intend to write books, though. From Boston on Sep 19, 1894, he wrote to Mrs. Arthur Smith: "I am at present lecturing in several places in Boston. What I want is to get a place where I can sit down and write down my thoughts. I have had enough of speaking; now I want to write. I think I will have to go to New York for it. Mrs. Guernsey was so kind to me, and she is ever willing to help me. I think I will go to her and sit down and write my book" (CW, 6. 268). In the same year, he wrote to Alasinga: "I am writing no book on Hinduism just now. I am simply jotting down my thoughts. I do not know if I shall publish them" (CW, 5. 61). A few months later, on May 6, 1895, he wrote to Alasinga again, this time sharing his insights on Vedanta and spirituality, concluding with: "I wish to write a book on this subject, therefore I wanted the three Bhashyas; but only one volume of the Ramanuja (Bhashya) has reached me as yet" (CW, 5. 82). On December 10, 1895, he wrote to Mrs. Ole Bull as well about his book project (see note 4 below).

3. See *Karma Yoga* (CW, 1. 25–118), *Raja Yoga* (CW, 1. 121–313), *Jñāna Yoga* (CW, 2. 57–288), and *Bhakti Yoga* (CW, 3. 31–100).

4. "I have begun to write in earnest, as I want to finish some text-books to form the basis of work when I am gone. I have to hurry through four little books before I go." Letter to Mrs. Bull. Written on Dec 10, 1895, from New York. CW, 6. 353.

5. See especially *Reminiscences of Swami Vivekananda* and Marie Louise Burke's *Swami Vivekananda in the West*, 6 vols. Both the titles are published by Advaita Ashrama, Kolkata.

6. There are a number of books, especially those written by monks of the Ramakrishna Order, which can be considered in a general sense to be commentaries on Vivekananda's teachings. But commentaries focusing on a specific text from Vivekananda's *Complete Works* and elaborating on specific passages from that text are yet to emerge.

7. Two classes were given on each of the following four Fridays: Dec 13 and 20, 1895, and Jan 3 and 10, 1896. The class for beginners was in the evening and the class for advanced students was in the morning. For inexplicable reasons, these talks don't appear in the *Complete Works* in chronological order. When read chronologically (first, the four talks to the beginners, and then, the four talks to the advanced students), it becomes much easier to see the gradual development of ideas and concepts. The recommended order of study is as follows: (1) Karma in Its Effect on Character (2) What Is Duty? (3) We Help Ourselves, Not the World (4) The Ideal of Karma Yoga (5) Each Is Great in His Own Place (6) The Secret of Work (7) Non-Attachment is Complete Self-Abnegation (8) Freedom.

8. Letter to E. T. Sturdy. Written on Aug 9, 1895, from New York. CW, 8. 349.

1. Yoga

1. These stages are traditionally said to be six (*ṣadvikāra*). Every living being exists (*asti*), takes birth (*jāyate*), grows (*vardhate*), undergoes changes (*vipariṇamate*), eventually begins to decline (*apakṣīyate*), and finally dies (*naśyati*).

2. "All the orthodox systems of Indian philosophy have one goal in view, the liberation of the soul through perfection. The method is by yoga. The word yoga covers an immense ground, but both the Samkhya and Vedanta Schools point to yoga in some form or other." CW, 1. 122. Yoga finds a place even in Buddhism and Jainism, which are considered heterodox and are not included in the orthodox schools (*āstika-darśana*) of Indian philosophy.

3. Bryant, Edwin, *The Yoga Sūtras of Patañjali* (New York: North Point Press, 2009), xx. See also Kramrisch, Stella, *The Presence of Śiva* (Princeton University Press, 1992), 10.

4. See, for instance, *Katha Upaniṣad* 6. 11–18, *Śvetāśvatara Upaniṣad* 2. 8–15, *Maitrī Upaniṣad* 6. 18—all of which belong to *Kṛṣṇa Yajur-Veda*. Several later texts, said to have emerged from the 9th to the 13th

centuries CE., also called themselves Upaniṣads and became collectively known as "minor" Upaniṣads. They are often categorized into thematic collections which indicate their dominant content. Among these are *Yoga Upaniṣads, Sannyāsa Upaniṣads, Śākta Upaniṣads, and Viṣṇu Upaniṣads.*

5. See especially the Mokṣa-dharma-parva (Book 12), Sanatsujātīya (Book 5) and Śāntiparva (Book 12) of the *Mahābhārata.* According to one count, the term appears around 900 times in the *Mahābhārata.* See John Brockington's "Yoga in the Mahābharata" in *Yoga: The Indian Tradition,* edited by Ian Whicher and David Carpenter (New York: Routledge Curzon, 2003). The *Gītā* speaks of yoga as "ancient" (4. 3) and references to yoga are spread throughout the *Gītā.*

6. See, for instance, *Yājñavalkya-Smṛti* (1. 8): "This alone is the highest *dharma,* that one should see the Ātman by yoga." Along with *Viṣṇu-Smṛti,* it also borrows verses from *Caraka-Saṃhitā.*

7. See especially the chapter on the embodied person ("Śarīrasthāna"), which also quotes from *Vaiśeṣika-sūtra* and *Sāṃkhya-Kārikā.*

8. Among the early texts of Haṭha Yoga are *Haṭha Yoga Pradīpikā* of Svātmārāma Yogīndra (14th century CE), *Gheraṇḍa Saṃhitā, Gorakṣa Saṃhitā* (attributed to Gorakṣanātha), and *Śiva Saṃhitā.* A contemporary and useful text for study is Mikel Burley's *Haṭha Yoga: Its Context, Theory and Practice* (Delhi: Motilal Banarsidass, 2000).

9. "The methods of spiritual realization have the generic name, 'yoga' (to join, to join ourselves to our reality). These yogas, though divided into various groups, can principally be classed into four; and as each is only a method of leading indirectly to the realization of the Absolute, they are suited to different temperaments." Written during Vivekananda's first visit to America, in response to questions put by a Western disciple. CW, 8. 152. See also CW, 9. 484, 5. 292.

10. It is possible to speak of three hearts: the physical heart, the emotional heart, and the spiritual heart. See Swami Tyagananda, "The Heart Beyond Hearts," in *Religion and the Arts,* Richard Kearney, ed. (Leiden: Brill, 2008), 12: 186–89.

11. This is not to suggest that Vivekananda invented these names. Yogas by these names did exist, but not in the sense that Vivekananda used them in his own scheme of four yogas, identifying each with a specific function of the human mind. His classification of yogas into four categories is his unique contribution to religion and spirituality.

12. "The grandest idea in Vedanta is that we may reach the same goal by different paths; and these paths I have generalized into four, viz. those of work, love, psychology, and knowledge. But you must, at the same time, remember that these divisions are not very marked

and quite exclusive of each other. Each blends into the other. But according to the type which prevails, we name the divisions. It is not that you can find people who have no other faculty than that of work, nor that you can find people who are no more than devoted worshippers only, nor that there are people who have no more than mere knowledge. These divisions are made in accordance with the type or the tendency that may be seen to prevail in a person. We have found that, in the end, all these four paths converge and become one. All religions and all methods of work and worship lead us to one and the same goal." *Karma Yoga:* "The Ideal of Karma Yoga." CW, 1. 108.

13. See, for instance, Vivekananda's letter of Nov 30, 1894, to his disciple, Dr. Nanjunda Rao: "Purity, patience, and perseverance are the three essentials to success and, above all, *love*." CW, 6. 281. Also, his letter of Oct 4, 1895, to his disciple, Christina Greenstidel: "Purity, patience, and perseverance overcome all obstacles. All great things must of necessity be slow." CW, 6. 344.

14. "Each soul is potentially divine. The goal is to manifest this divinity within, by controlling nature, external and internal. Do this either by work, or worship, or psychic control, or philosophy—by one or more or all of these—and be free. This is the whole of religion. Doctrines, or dogmas, or rituals, or books, or temples, or forms, are but secondary details." *Raja Yoga.* CW 1. 124.

15. "Each one of our yogas is fitted to make us perfect even without the help of the others, because they have all the same goal in view. The yogas of work, of wisdom, and of devotion are all capable of serving as direct and independent means for the attainment of *mokṣa*. 'Fools alone say that work and philosophy are different, not the learned.' The learned know that, though apparently different from each other, they at last lead to the same goal of human perfection." *Karma Yoga:* "Non-Attachment Is Complete Self-Abnegation." CW 1. 93.

16. "Intellectual, mystical, devotional, practical—make one the basis, but teach the others with it. Intellect must be balanced with love, the mystical nature with reason, while practice must form part of every method. Take every one where they stand and push them forward. Religious teaching must always be constructive, not destructive." *Inspired Talks:* Aug 5, 1895. CW, 7. 98.

17. Sri Ramakrishna's life is an eminent example of this, as we can see from his various spiritual practices.

18. "Develop every faculty as if it were the only one possessed, this is the true secret of so-called harmonious development." *Inspired Talks:* Aug 5, 1895. CW 7. 98.

2. Karma

1. "The word karma is derived from the Sanskrit *kr*, to do; all action is karma … In connection with metaphysics, it sometimes means the effects, of which our present actions were the causes. But in karma yoga we have simply to do with the word karma as meaning work…

   "Like fire in a piece of flint, knowledge exists in the mind; suggestion is the friction which brings it out. So with all our feelings and action—our tears and our smiles, our joys and our griefs, our weeping and our laughter, our curses and our blessings, our praises and our blames—every one of these we may find, if we calmly study our own selves, to have been brought out from within ourselves by so many blows. The result is what we are. All these blows taken together are called karma—work, action. Every mental and physical blow that is given to the soul, by which, as it were, fire is struck from it, and by which its own power and knowledge are discovered, is karma, this word being used in its widest sense. Thus we are all doing karma all the time. I am talking to you: that is karma. You are listening: that is karma. We breathe: that is karma. We walk: karma. Everything we do, physical or mental, is Karma, and it leaves its marks on us." *Karma Yoga:* "Karma in Its Effect on Character." CW 1. 27–29.

2. In common parlance, "work" often refers to one's professional life or career choice, but here it is used to mean any physical or mental action. Also, the work done by machines is not called karma, because it is not done by a conscious agent. So far as we know, a machine does not do its work with the awareness, "I am doing this work."

3. "No one can get anything unless he earns it. This is an eternal law. We may sometimes think it is not so, but in the long run we become convinced of it. A man may struggle all his life for riches; he may cheat thousands, but he finds at last that he did not deserve to become rich, and his life becomes a trouble and a nuisance to him. We may go on accumulating things for our physical enjoyment, but only what we earn is really ours. A fool may buy all the books in the world, and they will be in his library; but he will be able to read only those that he deserves to; and this deserving is produced by karma. Our karma determines what we deserve and what we can assimilate." *Karma Yoga:* "Karma in Its Effect on Character." CW 1. 31.

4. San Francisco: Apr 8, 1900. Lecture on "Is Vedanta the Future Religion?" CW, 8. 134.

5. "Animals are living upon plants, men upon animals and, worst of all, upon one another, the strong upon the weak. This is going on

everywhere … We hear every day many explanations, and are told that in the long run all will be good. Taking it for granted that this is possible, why should there be this diabolical way of doing good? Why cannot good be done through good, instead of through these diabolical methods? The descendants of the human beings of today will be happy; but why must there be all this suffering now?" London: Oct 15, 1896. *Jnana Yoga:* "Maya and Illusion." CW 2. 95.

6. Which does not mean God has nothing at all to do with karma. Philosophically, God (Sanskrit, *Īśvara*, "Supreme Ruler"), the principle of consciousness, is seen as the "giver of the fruits of karma" (*karmaphala-dātā*) according to each individual's karma. Everything other than God, including karma, is material, so a conscious principle is needed to animate karma and make it functional in the material world.

7. "Blame none for your own faults, stand upon your own feet, and take the whole responsibility upon yourselves. Say, 'This misery that I am suffering is of my own doing, and that very thing proves that it will have to be undone by me alone.' That which I created, I can demolish; that which is created by some one else I shall never be able to destroy. Therefore, stand up, be bold, be strong. Take the whole responsibility on your own shoulders, and know that you are the creator of your own destiny. All the strength and succor you want is within yourselves. Therefore, make your own future." New York: Jan 26, 1896. *Jnana Yoga:* "The Cosmos: The Microcosm." CW, 2. 225.

8. "Happiness presents itself before us, wearing the crown of sorrow on its head. Those who welcome it must also welcome sorrow." *Sayings and Utterances.* CW, 5. 419.

9. "Those that blame others—and, alas! the number of them is increasing every day—are generally miserable with helpless brains; they have brought themselves to that pass through their own mistakes and blame others, but this does not alter their position. It does not serve them in any way. This attempt to throw the blame upon others only weakens them the more." New York: Jan 26, 1896. *Jnana Yoga:* "The Cosmos: The Microcosm." CW, 2. 225.

10. While we can learn from *every* experience, it is often seen that we learn more from our bitter experiences than from the pleasant ones. "In studying the great characters the world has produced, I dare say, in the vast majority of cases, it would be found that it was misery that taught more than happiness, it was poverty that taught more than wealth, it was blows that brought out their inner fire more than praise." *Karma Yoga:* "Karma in Its Effect on Character." CW 1. 27.

11. "No one is to blame for our miseries but ourselves." Lecture on "What Is Religion?" CW, 1.342.

12. "We must learn that nothing can happen to us, unless we make ourselves susceptible to it. I have just said, no disease can come to me until the body is ready; it does not depend alone on the germs, but upon a certain predisposition which is already in the body. We get only that for which we are fitted. Let us give up our pride and understand this, that never is misery undeserved. There never has been a blow undeserved: there never has been an evil for which I did not pave the way with my own hands." Los Angeles: Jan 4, 1900. Lecture "Work and Its Secret." CW, 2.7.

13. "We Vedantists in every difficulty ought to ask the subjective question, 'Why do I see that?' 'Why can I not conquer this with love?'" Aug 8, 1896. Letter to J. J. Goodwin. CW, 8. 83.

14. Even if the idea is traced to a religious scripture, it would be viewed as a revelation by only those who accept and believe in that scripture. For others, what is in *their* scripture would be a revelation and everything else would be only a theory. The acceptance of scriptural testimony as revelation depends on faith and is not reached through objective evidence. For the nonreligious, everything that smacks of religion would be a "theory," and a superstitious theory, no less!

15. "The explanation of a thing must come from inside and not from outside. There had been the belief that, when a man threw up a stone and it fell, some demon dragged it down. Many occurrences which are really natural phenomena are attributed by people to unnatural beings. That a ghost dragged down the stone was an explanation that was not in the thing itself, it was an explanation from outside; but the second explanation of gravitation is something in the nature of the stone; the explanation is coming from inside. This tendency you will find throughout modern thought; in one word, what is meant by science is that the explanations of things are in their own nature, and that no external beings or existences are required to explain what is going on in the universe." London: Nov 18, 1896. Lecture on "Reason and Religion." CW, 1. 370–71.

16. "Thus, apart from the solid facts and truths that we may learn from religion, apart from the comforts that we may gain from it, religion, as a science, as a study, is the greatest and healthiest exercise that the human mind can have. This pursuit of the Infinite, this struggle to grasp the Infinite, this effort to get beyond the limitations of the senses—out of matter, as it were—and to evolve spiritually—this striving day and night to make the Infinite one with our being—this struggle itself is the grandest and most glorious that we can make." London: Jun 7, 1896. *Jnana Yoga:* "The Necessity of Religion." CW, 2.66.

17. "There never was a time when I was not, nor you, nor these kings. Nor will there ever be a time we all shall cease to be." *Gītā*, 2:12.

18. "Brahman is being, consciousness and infinity." *Taittirīya Upaniṣad*, 2.1.1.

    "That which is infinite is bliss. There is no bliss in the finite. It is the infinite alone which is bliss." *Chāndogya Upaniṣad*, 7.23.1.

19. "For you are dust, and to dust you shall return." *Genesis* 3:19

    "All mankind would perish together and man would return to dust." *Job* 34:15

    "For he knows how we were made; he remembers that we are dust." *Psalms* 103:14

    "All go to the same place; all come from dust, and to dust all return." *Ecclesiastes* 3:20

    "And the dust returns to the earth as it was, and the breath returns to God who gave it." *Ecclesiastes* 12:7

20. "This world is not our habitation, it is only one of the many stages through which we are passing." *Karma Yoga:* "The Secret of Work." CW, 1. 56.

21. Vivekananda disagreed with the idea that this world is some kind of a training ground where we come to learn our lessons. According to him, "This world is a circus ring in which we are the clowns tumbling." When asked, "Why do we tumble?" his answer was, "Because we *like* to tumble. When we get tired, we will quit." Camp Taylor, California: May 1900. *Conversations and Interviews.* CW, 9. 331.

22. This image is powerfully evoked in Buddha's *Lotus Sutra*, chapter 3.

23. See *The Gospel of Sri Ramakrishna* (Chennai: Sri Ramakrishna Math, 1980), 841. When Sri Ramakrishna was asked whether there is rebirth, he simply said that Krishna had confirmed in the *Gītā* that there is. Sri Ramakrishna did not give a simple yes or a no as his answer, because—strictly speaking—such positivity is not possible for a phenomenon that occurs in a relative (*vyāvahārika*) sense and is impossible in the absolute (*pāramārthika*) sense.

24. See *Saṁyutta Nikāya*, 45.165 and *Dīgha Nikāya*, 33.

25. "Having attained this temporary and joyless world, worship Me." *Gītā*, 9.33.

    "Having come to Me and reached the highest perfection, these great souls go beyond rebirth, which is impermanent and the abode of sorrow." *Gītā*, 8.15.

26. Krishna referred to this as "defect of sorrow" (*duḥkha-doṣa*) inherent in birth, death, old-age, and illness. See *Gītā*, 13.8.

27. "In enjoyment, there is the fear of disease; in social position, the fear of disrepute; in wealth, the fear of enemies; in honor, the fear of humiliation; in power, the fear of opponents; in beauty, the fear of old age; in scholarship, the fear of critics; in virtue, the fear of

gossip-mongers; in the body, the fear of death. Everything in this world associated with human beings is filled with fear. Renunciation alone leads to fearlessness. " Bhartṛhari, *Vairāgya-Śatakam*, 31.

28. "Why should the free, perfect, and pure being be thus under the thralldom of matter, is the next question. How can the perfect soul be deluded into the belief that it is imperfect? ... [The] answer is, 'I do not know.'" Chicago: Sep 19, 1893. "Paper on Hinduism" at the Parliament of Religions. (CW, 1. 9–10)

The answer "I do not know" is perfect for questions related to ignorance because the answer itself affirms the ignorance. It is impossible to have a positive and definitive answer to when, why or how something happened when, in fact, that something has never really happened. That is Vedanta's position. The one, infinite reality is always one and infinite even when, in our ignorance, we perceive it as finite and divided. It is a mystifying, bewildering situation. We cannot deny our perception because our experience affirms it. Nor can we confirm its validity because it completely contradicts the scripture (*śruti*), reason (*yukti*), and the experience (*anubhūti*) of those who are free from ignorance.

29. The key phrase here is "seems to be," meaning, it really is not. See the note above.

3. Detachment

1. "As desire increases, so increases the power of pleasure, so the power of pain." From notes discovered among Swami Vivekananda's papers. CW, 5. 429.

2. "Every moment of a [karma yogi's] life must be a realization, because he has to solve by mere work, without the help of doctrine or theory, the very same problem to which the Jñāni applies his reason and inspiration and the Bhakta his love." *Karma Yoga:* "The Ideal of Karma Yoga." CW, 1. 111.

3. "*Samskāra* can be translated very nearly by 'inherent tendency.' Using the simile of a lake for the mind, every ripple, every wave that rises in the mind, when it subsides, does not die out entirely, but leaves a mark and a future possibility of that wave coming out again. This mark, with the possibility of the wave reappearing, is what is called *samskāra*. Every work that we do, every movement of the body, every thought that we think, leaves such an impression on the mind-stuff, and even when such impressions are not obvious on the surface, they are sufficiently strong to work beneath the surface, subconsciously." *Karma Yoga:* "The Secret of Work." CW 1. 53–54.

4. "According to karma yoga, the action one has done cannot be destroyed until it has borne its fruit; no power in nature can stop it

from yielding its results. If I do an evil action, I must suffer for it; there is no power in this universe to stop or stay it. Similarly, if I do a good action, there is no power in the universe which can stop its bearing good results. The cause must have its effect; nothing can prevent or restrain this." *Karma Yoga:* "Non-Attachment Is Complete Self-Abnegation." CW, 1. 82.

5. "What we are every moment is determined by the sum total of these impressions on the mind. What I am just at this moment is the effect of the sum total of all the impressions of my past life. This is really what is meant by character; everyone's character is determined by the sum total of these impressions. If good impressions prevail, the character becomes good; if bad, it becomes bad.

"If a man continuously hears bad words, thinks bad thoughts, does bad actions, his mind will be full of bad impressions; and they will influence his thought and work without his being conscious of the fact. In fact, these bad impressions are always working, and their resultant must be evil, and that man will be a bad man; he cannot help it. The sum total of these impressions in him will create the strong motive power for doing bad actions. He will be like a machine in the hands of his impressions, and they will force him to do evil.

"Similarly, if a man thinks good thoughts and does good works, the sum total of these impressions will be good; and they, in a similar manner, will force him to do good even in spite of himself. When a man has done so much good work and thought so many good thoughts that there is an irresistible tendency in him to do good in spite of himself and even if he wishes to do evil, his mind, as the sum total of his tendencies, will not allow him to do so; the tendencies will turn him back; he is completely under the influence of the good tendencies. When such is the case, a man's good character is said to be established." *Karma Yoga:* "The Secret of Work." CW, 1. 54–55.

6. "If you take the character of any man, it really is but the aggregate of tendencies, the sum total of the bent of his mind." *Karma Yoga:* "Karma in Its Effect on Character." CW, 1. 27

It is karma that shapes our character and it is character that controls the will: "All the actions that we see in the world, all the movements in human society, all the works that we have around us, are simply the display of thought, the manifestation of the human will … and this will is caused by character, and character is manufactured by karma. As is karma, so is the manifestation of the will." *Karma Yoga:* "Karma in Its Effect on Character." CW, 1. 30.

7. Desires can be problematic but not *all* desires. There are always exceptions. Exceptions, in fact, prove the rule. As Sri Ramakrishna often pointed out, greens can be tough on some stomachs and an

excess of sweets can affect health, but *hinche* greens and sugar candy are exceptions because of their medicinal properties. See M, *The Gospel of Sri Ramakrishna* (Chennai: Sri Ramakrishna Math, 1980), 678, 680, 938. The botanical name for *hinche* green is *Enhydra Fluctuance Lour* and it belongs to the plant family of *Compositae*.

8. "Heaven is a mere superstition arising from desire, and desire is a yoke, a degeneration." New York: Jul 5, 1895. *Inspired Talks*. CW, 7. 34.

   "This whole universe is only one speck of the infinite being; and all our laws, our bondages, our joys and our sorrows, our happinesses and our expectations, are only within this small universe; all our progression and digression are within its small compass. So you see how childish it is to expect a continuation of this universe—the creation of our minds—and to expect to go to heaven, which after all must mean only a repetition of this world that we know. You see at once that it is an impossible and childish desire to make the whole of infinite existence conform to the limited and conditioned existence which we know." *Karma Yoga:* "Freedom." CW, 1. 96.

9. "To acquire freedom we have to get beyond the limitations of this universe; it cannot be found here. Perfect equilibrium, or what the Christians call the peace that passeth all understanding, cannot be had in this universe, nor in heaven, nor in any place where our mind and thoughts can go, where the senses can feel, or which the imagination can conceive. No such place can give us that freedom, because all such places would be within our universe, and it is limited by space, time, and causation." *Karma Yoga:* "Freedom." CW, 1. 97.

10. "All the worlds, including the realm of Brahmā, are subject to return." *Gītā*, 8.16.

11. "Strike off thy fetters! Bonds that bind thee down,
    Of shining gold, or darker, baser ore;
    Love, hate—good, bad—and all the dual throng,
    Know, slave is slave, caressed or whipped, not free;
    For fetters, though of gold, are not less strong to bind;
    Then off with them, Sannyāsin bold! Say —
    Om Tat Sat, Om!"
    New York: Jul 1895. Poem titled "The Song of the Sannyāsin." CW, 4. 393.

    "Liberation means entire freedom—freedom from the bondage of good, as well as from the bondage of evil. A golden chain is as much a chain as an iron one. There is a thorn in my finger, and I use another to take the first one out; and when I have taken it out, I throw both of them aside; I have no necessity for keeping the second thorn, because both are thorns after all. So the bad tendencies are to be counteracted by the good ones, and the bad impressions on the mind should be removed by the fresh waves of good ones, until all that is evil almost disappears, or is subdued and held in control in a corner of the mind; but after that, the good tendencies have also to be conquered." *Karma Yoga:* The Secret of Work." CW, 1. 55–56.

12. "That which you see as different from *dharma*, different from *adharma*, different from all this cause and effect, and different from the past and the future—tell me That." *Kaṭha Upaniṣad*, 1.2.14 .

13. "Work (done as *yoga*) leads to purification of the heart." Śaṅkarācārya, *Vivekacuḍāmañi*, 11.

14. "Wherever there is attachment, the clinging to the things of the world, you must know that it is all physical attraction between sets of particles of matter—something that attracts two bodies nearer and nearer all the time and, if they cannot get near enough, produces pain; but where there is *real* love, it does not rest on physical attachment at all. Such lovers may be a thousand miles away from one another, but their love will be all the same; it does not die, and will never produce any painful reaction." *Karma Yoga:* "The Secret of Work." CW, 1. 58–59.

15. "The highest point of all is to see no difference between lover and beloved. You may remember, perhaps, the old Persian story, of how a lover came and knocked at the door of the beloved and was asked, 'Who are you?' He answered, 'It is I,' and there was no response. A second time he came, and exclaimed, 'I am here,' but the door was not opened. The third time he came, and the voice asked from inside, 'Who is there?' He replied, 'I am thyself, my beloved,' and the door opened. So is the relation between God and ourselves. He is in everything. He is everything. Every man and woman is the palpable, blissful, living God. Who says God is unknown? Who says God is to be searched after? We have found God eternally. We have been living in God eternally." London: Nov 12, 1896. Lecture on "Practical Vedanta." CW, 2. 326–27. See also CW, 8. 221.

16. "Suppose a man loves a woman; he wishes to have her all to himself and feels extremely jealous about her every movement; he wants her to sit near him, to stand near him, and to eat and move at his bidding. He is a slave to her and wishes to have her as his slave. That is not love; it is a kind of morbid affection of the slave, insinuating itself as love. It cannot be love, because it is painful; if she does not do what he wants, it brings him pain. With love there is no painful reaction; love only brings a reaction of bliss; if it does not, it is not love; it is mistaking something else for love. When you have succeeded in loving your husband, your wife, your children, the whole world, the universe, in such a manner that there is no

reaction of pain or jealousy, no selfish feeling, then you are in a fit state to be unattached." *Karma Yoga:* "The Secret of Work." CW, 1. 58.

17. "Work through love! The word 'love' is very difficult to understand; love never comes until there is freedom. There is no true love possible in the slave." *Karma Yoga:* "The Secret of Work." CW, 1. 57.

18. "Every act of love brings happiness; there is no act of love which does not bring peace and blessedness as its reaction. Real existence, real knowledge, and real love are eternally connected with one another, the three in one: where one of them is, the others also must be; they are the three aspects of the One without a second—the Existence-Knowledge-Bliss. When that existence becomes relative, we see it as the world; that knowledge becomes in its turn modified into the knowledge of the things of the world; and that bliss forms the foundation of all true love known to the heart of man. Therefore true love can never react so as to cause pain either to the lover or to the beloved." *Karma Yoga:* "The Secret of Work." CW, 1. 57–58.

19. Śaṅkarācārya's commentary on *Kaṭhopaniṣad*, 1.1.2.

20. "Brahman is the Ear of the ear, Mind of the mind, the Speech of speech, the Life of life, and the Eye of the eyes." *Kena Upaniṣad*, 1.2.

21. "There is one who is the eternal reality among non-eternal objects, the one truly conscious being among apparently conscious objects, and who, though nondual, fulfills the desires of many. Eternal peace belongs to the wise, who perceive this being within themselves." *Katha Upaniṣad*, 2.2.13.

22. 2 Corinthians 3:6.

23. "Karma yoga teaches us how to work for work's sake, unattached, without caring who is helped, and what for. The karma yogi works because it is his nature, because he feels that it is good for him to do so, and he has no object beyond that. His position in this world is that of a giver, and he never cares to receive anything. He knows that he is giving, and does not ask for anything in return and, therefore, he eludes the grasp of misery. The grasp of pain, whenever it comes, is the result of the reaction of 'attachment'." New York: Jan 12, 1896. Lecture on "The Ideal of a Universal Religion." CW, 2. 392.

"When work is done for work's sake, without attachment and without seeking fruit, such renunciation is considered *sāttvika.*" *Gītā*, 18.9.

24. "People work with various motives. There cannot be work without motive. Some people want to get fame, and they work for fame. Others want money, and they work for money. Others want to have power, and they work for power. Others want to get to heaven, and

they work for the same. Others want to leave a name when they die, … [and they] work for that … Others work as a penance; do all sorts of wicked things, then erect a temple, or give something to the priests to buy them off and obtain from them a passport to heaven. They think that this kind of beneficence will clear them and they will go scot-free in spite of their sinfulness. Such are some of the various motives for work." *Karma Yoga:* "Karma in Its Effect on Character." CW, 1. 31–32.

25. "When the idea of doing good becomes a part of our very being, then we will not seek for any motive outside. Let us do good because it is good to do good. He who does good work even in order to get to heaven binds himself down, says the karma yogi. Any work that is done with any the least selfish motive, instead of making us free, forges one more chain for our feet." *Karma Yoga:* "The Ideal of Karma Yoga." CW, 1. 116.

26. "Work for work's sake. There are some who are really the salt of the earth in every country and who work for work's sake, who do not care for name, or fame, or even to go to heaven. They work just because good will come of it. There are others who do good to the poor and help mankind from still higher motives, because they believe in doing good and love good." *Karma Yoga:* "Karma in Its Effect on Character." CW, 1. 32.

27. "When you give something to a man and expect nothing—do not even expect the man to be grateful—his ingratitude will not tell upon you, because you never expected anything, never thought you had any right to anything in the way of a return. You gave him what he deserved; his own karma got it for him; your karma made you the carrier thereof. Why should you be proud of having given away something? You are the porter that carried the money or other kind of gift, and the world deserved it by its own karma. Where is then the reason for pride in you? There is nothing very great in what you give to the world." *Karma Yoga:* "Non-Attachment Is Complete Self-Abnegation." CW, 1. 90.

28. "Now you see what Karma-Yoga means; even at the point of death to help any one, without asking questions. Be cheated millions of times and never ask a question, and never think of what you are doing. Never vaunt of your gifts to the poor or expect their grati-tude, but rather be grateful to them for giving you the occasion of practicing charity to them." *Karma Yoga:* "The Secret of Work." CW 1. 62.

29. "Ordinarily if a man goes out into the street and shoots down another man, he is apt to feel sorry for it, thinking that he has done wrong. But if the very same man, as a soldier in his regiment, kills not one but twenty, he is certain to feel glad and think that he has done his duty remarkably well. Therefore we see that it is not the

thing done that defines a duty. To give an objective definition of duty is thus entirely impossible. Yet there is duty from the subjective side. Any action that makes us go Godward is a good action, and is our duty; any action that makes us go downward is evil, and is not our duty.

"From the subjective standpoint we may see that certain acts have a tendency to exalt and ennoble us, while certain other acts have a tendency to degrade and to brutalize us. But it is not possible to make out with certainty which acts have which kind of tendency in relation to all persons, of all sorts and conditions. There is, however, only one idea of duty which has been universally accepted by all mankind, of all ages and sects and countries, and that has been summed up in a Sanskrit aphorism thus: 'Do not injure any being; not injuring any being is virtue, injuring any being is sin.'" *Karma Yoga:* "What Is Duty?" CW 1. 64.

30. *Muṇḍaka Upaniṣad,* 3.1.6.

31. "Three things are necessary to make every man great, every nation great:

    1. Conviction of the powers of goodness.

    2. Absence of jealousy and suspicion.

    3. Helping all who are trying to be and do good."

    Jan 29, 1894. Letter to Haridas Viharidas Desai. CW, 8. 299.

32. "Treating alike pain and pleasure, gain and loss, victory and defeat, then get ready for the battle. In this way you will incur no sin." *Gītā,* 2.38.

33. "Heed then no more how body lives or goes,

    Its task is done. Let karma float it down;

    Let one put garlands on, another kick

    This frame; say naught. No praise or blame can be

    Where praiser praised, and blamer blamed are one.

    Thus be thou calm, Sannyāsin bold!

    Say — "Om Tat Sat, Om!"

    New York: Jul 1895. Poem titled "The Song of the Sannyāsin. CW, 4. 394.

34. "There is another way in which this idea of mercy and selfless charity can be put into practice; that is, by looking upon work as 'worship' in case we believe in a personal God. Here we give up all the fruits our work unto God, and worshipping him thus, we have no right to expect anything from others for the work we do. God himself works incessantly and is ever without attachment. Just as water cannot wet the lotus leaf, so work cannot bind the unselfish person by giving rise to attachment to results. The selfless and unattached man may live in the very heart of a crowded and sinful city; he will not be touched by sin." *Karma Yoga:* "The Secret of Work." CW, 1. 59–60. See also *Gītā,* 9.27.

35. "For whatever good work we may do, let us not claim any praise or benefit. It is the Lord's. Give up the fruits unto him. Let us stand aside and think that we are only servants obeying the Lord, our Master, and that every impulse for action comes from him every moment. Whatever thou worshippest, whatever thou perceivest, whatever thou doest, give up all unto him and be at rest. Let us be at peace, perfect peace, with ourselves, and give up our whole body and mind and everything as an eternal sacrifice unto the Lord." *Karma Yoga:* "Freedom." CW, 1. 102.

36. "Look upon every man, woman, and every one as God. You cannot help anyone, you can only serve: serve the children of God, serve God himself, if you have the privilege. If the Lord grants that you can help any one of his children, blessed you are. Do not think too much of yourselves. Blessed you are that that privilege was given to you when others had it not. Do it only as a worship. I should see God in the poor, and it is for my salvation that I go and worship them. The poor and the miserable are for our salvation, so that we may serve God, coming in the shape of the diseased, coming in the shape of the lunatic, the leper, and the sinner! Bold are my words; and let me repeat that it is the greatest privilege in our life that we are allowed to serve God in all these shapes." Chennai: Jan 1897. Lecture on "Vedanta in Its Application to Indian Life." CW, 3. 246–47.

37. "Doctrines have been expounded enough. There are books by the million. Oh, for an ounce of practice!" New York: Aug 9, 1895. Letter to E. T. Sturdy. CW, 8. 349.

38. "The whole scope of all systems of yoga (and each religion represents one) is to remove ignorance and allow the Ātman to restore its own nature. The chief helps in this liberation are *abhyāsa* and *vairāgya*. *Vairāgya* is non-attachment to life, because it is the will to enjoy that brings all this bondage in its train; and *abhyāsa* is constant practice of any one of the yogas." From a letter in response to questions put by a Western disciple. CW, 8. 152.

4. Practice

1. "Faith, faith, faith in ourselves, faith, faith in God—this is the secret of greatness. If you have faith in all the three hundred and thirty millions of your mythological gods, and in all the gods which foreigners have now and again introduced into your midst, and still have no faith in yourselves, there is no salvation for you. Have faith in yourselves, and stand up on that faith and be strong. That is what we need." Kumbakonam: 1897. Lecture on "The Mission of Vedanta." CW, 3. 190.

"Our first duty is not to hate ourselves, because to advance we must have faith in ourselves first and then in God. He who has no faith in himself can never have faith in God." *Karma Yoga:* "Each Is Great in His Own Place." CW, 1. 38.

2. See Swami Saradananda, *Sri Ramakrishna the Great Master,* tr. Swami Jagadananda (Chennai: Sri Ramakrishna Math, 1984), 815, 901.

3. "Every act of selfishness or thought of selfishness makes us attached to something, and immediately we are made slaves. Each wave in the mind that says 'I and mine' immediately puts a chain round us and makes us slaves; and the more we say 'I and mine,' the more slavery grows, the more misery increases … Never say 'mine.' Whenever we say a thing is 'mine,' misery will immediately come. Do not even say 'my child' in your mind. Possess the child, but do not say 'mine.' If you do, then will come the misery. Do not say 'my house,' do not say 'my body.' The whole difficulty is there. The body is neither yours, nor mine, nor anybody's. These bodies are coming and going by the laws of nature, but we are free, standing as witness. This body is no more free than a picture or a wall. Why should we be attached so much to a body? If somebody paints a picture, he does it and passes on. Do not project that tentacle of selfishness, 'I must possess it.' As soon as that is projected, misery will begin." *Karma Yoga:* "Freedom." CW, 1. 100–101.

4. The *Gītā* (14.24) sees this practice of remaining unaffected by praise or blame as a discipline for one who wants to break free from the karma chain.

5. "My master used to say, 'Look upon your children as a nurse does.' The nurse will take your baby and fondle it and play with it and behave towards it as gently as if it were her own child; but as soon as you give her notice to quit, she is ready to start off bag and baggage from the house. Everything in the shape of attachment is forgotten; it will not give the ordinary nurse the least pang to leave your children and take up other children. Even so are you to be with all that you consider your own. You are the nurse, and if you believe in God, believe that all these things which you consider yours are really his." *Karma Yoga:* "Non-Attachment Is Complete Self-Abnegation." CW, 1. 88–89.

6. "Karma yogis must throw this idea of duty overboard. There is no duty for you and me. Whatever you have to give to the world, do give by all means, but not as a duty. Do not take any thought of that. Be not compelled. Why should you be compelled? Everything that you do under compulsion goes to build up attachment. Why should you have any duty? Resign everything unto God. In this tremendous fiery furnace where the fire of duty scorches every-

body, drink this cup of nectar and be happy." *Karma Yoga:* "Freedom." CW, 1. 104.

7. "What about this marvelous experience of standing alone, discarding all help, breasting the storms of life, of working without any sense of recompense, without any sense of putrid duty, and of working a whole life, joyful, free—not goaded on to work like slaves by false human love or ambition?" "The Social Conference Address." CW, 4. 307.

8. "Duty is seldom sweet. It is only when love greases its wheels that it runs smoothly. It is a continuous friction otherwise. How else could parents do their duties to their children, husbands to their wives, and vice versa? Do we not meet with cases of friction every day in our lives? Duty is sweet only through love, and love shines in freedom alone." *Karma Yoga:* "What Is Duty?" CW, 1. 67.

9. "The whole gist of this teaching is that you should work like a master and not as a slave. Work incessantly, but do not do slave's work. Do you not see how everybody works? Nobody can be altogether at rest. Ninety-nine per cent of mankind work like slaves, and the result is misery. It is all selfish work. Work through freedom!" *Karma Yoga:* "The Secret of Work." CW, 1. 57.

10. "No man is to be judged by the mere nature of his duties, but all should be judged by the manner and the spirit in which they perform them." *Karma Yoga:* "What Is Duty?" CW, 1. 66.

11. "Later on we shall find that even this idea of duty undergoes change, and that the greatest work is done only when there is no selfish motive to prompt it. Yet it is work through the sense of duty that leads us to work without any idea of duty. When work will become worship—nay, something higher—then will work be done for its own sake." *Karma Yoga:* "What Is Duty?" CW, 1. 66.

12. "Yet we may see that this peculiar sense of duty is very often a great cause of misery. Duty becomes a disease with us. It drags us ever forward. It catches hold of us and makes our whole life miserable. It is the bane of human life. This duty, this idea of duty is the midday summer sun which scorches the innermost soul of mankind. Look at those poor slaves to duty! Duty leaves them no time to say prayers, no time to bathe. Duty is ever on them. They go out and work. Duty is on them! They come home and think of the work for the next day. Duty is on them! It is living a slave's life, at last dropping down in the street and dying in harness, like a horse. This is duty as it is understood." *Karma Yoga:* "Freedom." CW, 1. 103.

13. "It is the worker who is attached to results that grumbles about the nature of the duty which has fallen to his lot. To the unattached worker all duties are equally good, and form efficient instruments with which selfishness and sensuality may be killed, and the

freedom of the soul secured. We are all apt to think too highly of ourselves. Our duties are determined by our deserts to a much larger extent than we are willing to grant. Competition rouses envy, and it kills the kindliness of the heart. To the grumbler all duties are distasteful; nothing will ever satisfy him, and his whole life is doomed to prove a failure. Let us work on, doing as we go whatever happens to be our duty, and being ever ready to put our shoulders to the wheel. Then surely shall we see the Light!" *Karma Yoga:* "What Is Duty?" CW, 1. 71.

14. "It is easy for people to think that they can understand everything. But when it comes to practical experience, they find that abstract ideas are often very hard to comprehend. Therefore symbols are of great help, and we cannot dispense with the symbolical method of putting things before us. From time immemorial symbols have been used by all kinds of religions. In one sense we cannot think but in symbols. Words themselves are symbols of thought … Language is not the result of convention; it is not that people ever agreed to represent certain ideas by certain words; there never was an idea without a corresponding word or a word without a corresponding idea. Ideas and words are in their nature inseparable. The symbols to represent ideas may be sound symbols or color symbols … The study and practice of these things form naturally a part of karma yoga." *Karma Yoga:* "We Help Ourselves, Not the World." CW, 1. 72–74.

15. "There are many other aspects of this science of work. One among them is to know the relation between thought and word, and what can be achieved by the power of the word … I am talking to you. I am not touching you. The pulsations of the air caused by my speaking go into your ear, they touch your nerves and produce effects in your minds. You cannot resist this. What can be more wonderful than this? One man calls another a fool, and at this the other stands up and clenches his fist and lands a blow on his nose. Look at the power of the word! There is a woman weeping and miserable; another woman comes along and speaks to her a few gentle words, the doubled up frame of the weeping woman becomes straightened at once, her sorrow is gone and she already begins to smile. Think of the power of words! They are a great force in higher philosophy as well as in common life. Day and night we manipulate this force without thought and without inquiry. To know the nature of this force and to use it well is also a part of karma yoga." *Karma Yoga:* "We Help Ourselves, Not the World." CW, 1. 74–75.

16. New York: Jun 26, 1895. *Inspired Talks.* CW, 7. 16.

17. "Even idiots may stand up to hear themselves praised, and cowards assume the attitude of the brave when everything is sure to turn

out well, but the true hero works in silence." Washington: Oct 27, 1894. Letter to Alasinga Perumal. CW, 5. 51–52.

18. The five senses of knowledge are those that facilitate hearing, touch, sight, taste, and smell. The five senses of action are those that facilitate speech, excretion and reproduction, and the functions of hands and feet.

19. "Leave the fruits alone. Why care for results? If you wish to help a man, never think what that man's attitude should be towards you. If you want to do a great or a good work, do not trouble to think what the result will be." *Karma Yoga:* "Karma in Its Effect on Character." CW 1. 33–34.

   "In the world take always the position of the giver. Give everything and look for no return. Give love, give help, give service, give any little thing you can, but keep out barter. Make no conditions, and none will be imposed. Let us give out of our own bounty, just as God gives to us." New York: Jun 19, 1895. *Inspired Talks.* CW, 7. 5.

   "We get caught. How? Not by what we give, but by what we expect ... There is no misery where there is no want. Desire, want, is the father of all misery. Desires are bound by the laws of success and failure. Desires must bring misery.

   "The great secret of true success, of true happiness, then, is this: the man who asks for no return, the perfectly unselfish man, is the most successful ... Ask nothing; want nothing in return. Give what you have to give; it will come back to you—but do not think of that now, it will come back multiplied a thousandfold—but the attention must not be on that. Yet have the power to give: give, and there it ends." Los Angeles: Jan 4, 1900. Lecture on "Work and Its Secret." CW 2. 4–5. See also *Gītā,* 2.47.

20. See *Gītā,* 2.47.

21. "Karma yoga makes a science of work. You learn by it how best to utilize all the workings of this world. Work is inevitable: it must be so, but we should work to the highest purpose. Karma yoga makes us admit that this world is a world of five minutes, that it is a something we have to pass through; and that freedom is not here, but is only to be found beyond ... Karma yoga shows the process, the secret, and the method of doing it to the best advantage." *Karma Yoga:* "Freedom." CW, 1. 99–100.

   "With regard to karma yoga, the *Gītā* (2.50) says that it is doing work with cleverness and as a science; by knowing how to work, one can obtain the greatest results." *Karma Yoga:* "Karma in Its Effect on Character." CW, 1. 31.

5. Freedom

1. See Sadānanda Yogīndra, *Vedānta Sāra*, 30.
2. "Pleasure is not the goal but knowledge. Pleasure and happiness come to an end. It is a mistake to suppose that pleasure is the goal. The cause of all the miseries we have in the world is that we foolishly think pleasure to be the ideal to strive for. After a time we find that it is not happiness, but knowledge, towards which we are going, and that both pleasure and pain are great teachers, and that we learn as much from evil as from good." *Karma Yoga:* "Karma in Its Effect on Character." CW, 1. 27.
3. "I have already tried to point out that goal. It is freedom as I understand it. Everything that we perceive around us is struggling towards freedom, from the atom to the man, from the insentient, lifeless particle of matter to the highest existence on earth, the human soul. The whole universe is in fact the result of this struggle for freedom. In all combinations every particle is trying to go on its own way, to fly from the other particles, but the others are holding it in check. Our earth is trying to fly away from the sun, and the moon from the earth. Everything has a tendency to infinite dispersion.

   "All that we see in the universe has for its basis this one struggle towards freedom; it is under the impulse of this tendency that the saint prays and the robber robs. When the line of action taken is not a proper one, we call it evil; and when the manifestation of it is proper and high, we call it good. But the impulse is the same, the struggle towards freedom. The saint is oppressed with the knowledge of his condition of bondage, and he wants to get rid of it; so he worships God. The thief is oppressed with the idea that he does not possess certain things, and he tries to get rid of that want, to obtain freedom from it; so he steals.

   "Freedom is the one goal of all nature, sentient or insentient. Consciously or unconsciously, everything is struggling towards that goal. The freedom which the saint seeks is very different from that which the robber seeks. The freedom loved by the saint leads him to the enjoyment of infinite, unspeakable bliss, while that on which the robber has set his heart only forges other bonds for his soul." *Karma Yoga:* "The Ideal of Karma Yoga." CW, 1. 108–109.
4. "There is to be found in every religion the manifestation of this struggle towards freedom. It is the groundwork of all morality, of unselfishness, which means getting rid of the idea that we are the same as our little body. When we see a man doing good work, helping others, it means that he cannot be confined within the limited circle of 'me and mine.' There is no limit to this getting out of selfishness. All the great systems of ethics preach absolute

unselfishness as the goal." *Karma Yoga:* "The Ideal of Karma Yoga." CW, 1. 109.

5. "The question has been raised as to from whom this universe comes, in whom it rests, and to whom it goes; and the answer has been given that from freedom it comes, in bondage it rests, and goes back into that freedom again." *Karma Yoga:* "Freedom." CW, 1. 96.

6. "You must remember that freedom of the soul is the goal of all Yogas, and each one equally leads to the same result. By work alone men may get to where Buddha got largely by meditation or Christ by prayer. Buddha was a working Jñāni, Christ was a Bhakta, but the same goal was reached by both of them." *Karma Yoga:* "The Secret of Work." CW, 1. 55.

7. "But we have to begin from the beginning, to take up the works as they come to us and slowly make ourselves more unselfish every day. We must do the work and find out the motive power that prompts us. Almost without exception, in the first years, we shall find that our motives are always selfish. But gradually this selfishness will melt by persistence, till at last will come the time when we shall be able to do really unselfish work." *Karma Yoga:* "Karma in Its Effect on Character." CW, 1. 34–35.

8. "Unselfishness is more paying, only people have not the patience to practice it. It is more paying from the point of view of health also. Love, truth, and unselfishness are not merely moral figures of speech, but they form our highest ideal, because in them lies such a manifestation of power." *Karma Yoga:* "Karma in Its Effect on Character." CW, 1. 32.

9. "The ideal man is he who, in the midst of the greatest silence and solitude, finds the intensest activity, and in the midst of the intensest activity finds the silence and solitude of the desert. He has learnt the secret of restraint, he has controlled himself. He goes through the streets of a big city with all its traffic, and his mind is as calm as if he were in a cave, where not a sound could reach him; and he is intensely working all the time. That is the ideal of karma yoga, and if you have attained to that you have really learnt the secret of work." *Karma Yoga:* "Karma in Its Effect on Character." CW, 1. 34.

10. "The greatest people in the world have passed away unknown. The Buddhas and the Christs that we know are but second-rate heroes in comparison with the greatest of whom the world knows nothing. Hundreds of these unknown heroes have lived in every country working silently. Silently they live and silently they pass away; and in time their thoughts find expression in Buddhas or Christs, and it is these latter that become known to us. The highest men do not seek to get any name or fame from their knowledge. They leave

their ideas to the world; they put forth no claims for themselves and establish no schools or systems in their name. Their whole nature shrinks from such a thing. ...

"The highest men are calm, silent, and unknown. They are the ones who really know the power of thought. They are sure that, even if they go into a cave and close the door and simply think five true thoughts and then pass away, these five thoughts of theirs will live through eternity. Indeed such thoughts will penetrate through the mountains, cross the oceans, and travel through the world. They will enter deep into human hearts and brains and raise up men and women who will give them practical expression in the workings of human life." *Karma Yoga:* "Freedom." CW 1. 105–106.

11. "If Buddha was great in life, he was also great in death ... An old man came and sat near him—he had walked miles and miles to see the Master—and Buddha taught him. When he found a disciple weeping, he reproved him, saying, 'What is this? Is this the result of all my teaching? Let there be no false bondage, no dependence on me, no false glorification of this passing personality. The Buddha is not a person; he is a realization. Work out your own salvation.' Even when dying, he would not claim any distinction for himself. I worship him for that. What you call Buddhas and Christs are only the names of certain states of realization. Of all the teachers of the world, he was the one who taught us most to be self-reliant, who freed us not only from the bondages of our false selves but from dependence on the invisible being or beings called God." San Francisco: Mar 18, 1900. Lecture on "Buddha's Message to the World." CW, 8. 104–105.

12. "Buddha is the only prophet who said, 'I do not care to know your various theories about God. What is the use of discussing all the subtle doctrines about the soul? Do good and be good. And this will take you to freedom and to whatever truth there is.' He was, in the conduct of his life, absolutely without personal motives; and what man worked more than he? Show me in history one character who has soared so high above all. The whole human race has produced but one such character, such high philosophy, such wide sympathy. This great philosopher, preaching the highest philosophy, yet had the deepest sympathy for the lowest of animals, and never put forth any claims for himself. He is the ideal karma yogi, acting entirely without motive, and the history of humanity shows him to have been the greatest man ever born; beyond compare the greatest combination of heart and brain that ever existed, the greatest soul-power that has ever been manifested. He is the first great reformer the world has seen. He was the first who dared to say, 'Believe not because some old manuscripts are produced, believe not because it is your national belief, because you have been

made to believe it from your childhood; but reason it all out, and after you have analyzed it, then, if you find that it will do good to one and all, believe it, live up to it, and help others to live up to it.' He works best who works without any motive, neither for money, nor for fame, nor for anything else; and when a man can do that, he will be a Buddha, and out of him will come the power to work in such a manner as will transform the world. This man represents the very highest ideal of karma yoga." *Karma Yoga:* "The Ideal of Karma Yoga." CW, 1. 117–18.

About the Author

Swami Tyagananda, a monk of the Ramakrishna Order since 1976, is the head of the Vedanta Society in Boston, and is the Hindu Chaplain at Harvard and MIT. He has written, translated and edited twelve books, including *Monasticism: Ideals and Traditions* (1991), *The Essence of the Gita* (2000), *Interpreting Ramakrishna* (2011), and *Knowing the Knower: A Manual of Jnana Yoga* (2017).

facebook.com/VedantaBoston
twitter.com/SwamiTyagananda

.

Printed in Great Britain
by Amazon